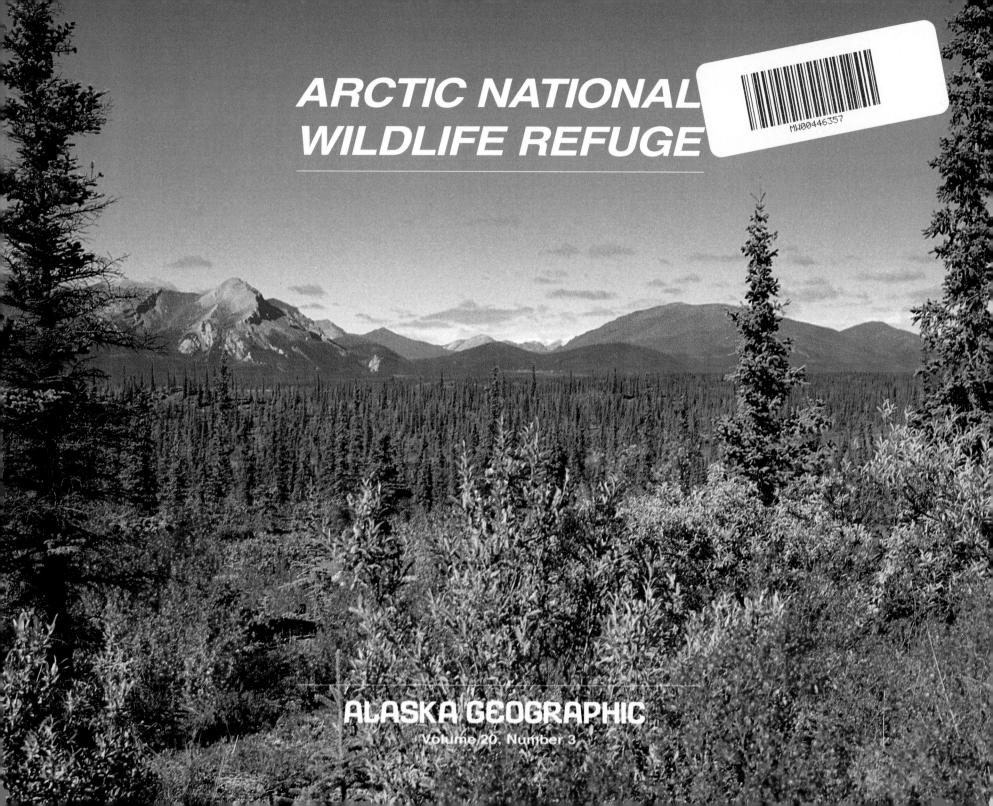

ARCTIC NATIONAL
WILDLIFE REFUGE

ALASKA GEOGRAPHIC

Volume 20, Number 3

The Alaska Geographic Society

To teach many more to better know and more wisely use our natural resources

EDITOR
Penny Rennick

PRODUCTION DIRECTOR
Kathy Doogan

STAFF WRITER
L.J. Campbell

BUSINESS & CIRCULATION MANAGER
Kevin Kerns

CUSTOMER SERVICE REPRESENTATIVE
Patty Bliss

POSTMASTER: Send address changes to
ALASKA GEOGRAPHIC®
P.O. Box 93370
Anchorage, Alaska 99509-3370

ISBN: 1-56661-012-5 (paper); 1-56661-013-3 (hardback)

PRICE TO NON-MEMBERS THIS ISSUE: $18.95

BOARD OF DIRECTORS
Richard Carlson, Kathy Doogan, Penny Rennick

Robert A. Henning, *President Emeritus*

ALASKA GEOGRAPHIC® (ISSN 0361-1353) is published quarterly by The Alaska Geographic Society, 639 West International Airport Road, Unit 38, Anchorage, AK 99518. Second-class postage paid at Anchorage, Alaska, and additional mailing offices. Copyright © 1993 by The Alaska Geographic Society. All rights reserved. Registered trademark: Alaska Geographic, ISSN 0361-1353; Key title Alaska Geographic.

THE ALASKA GEOGRAPHIC SOCIETY is a non-profit organization exploring new frontiers of knowledge across the lands of the Polar Rim, putting the geography book back in the classroom, exploring new methods of teaching and learning—sharing in the excitement of discovery in man's wonderful new world north of 51°16´.

SOCIETY MEMBERS receive *ALASKA GEOGRAPHIC*®, a quality magazine that devotes each quarterly issue to monographic in-depth coverage of a northern geographic region or resource-oriented subject.

MEMBERSHIP in The Alaska Geographic Society costs $39 per year, $49 to non-U.S. addresses. ($31.20 of the $39 is for a one-year subscription to *ALASKA GEOGRAPHIC*®.) Order from The Alaska Geographic Society, P.O. Box 93370, Anchorage, AK 99509-3370; phone (907) 562-0164, fax (907) 562-0479.

ABOUT THIS ISSUE: By mid-1993 the fate of the Arctic National Wildlife Refuge was still not known. Whether the refuge would remain as it was, have portions of its coastal plain opened to oil development or have the bulk of its acreage not already designated wilderness reclassified to wilderness status was yet to be determined. But readers have inquired about this controversial corner of northeastern Alaska so it seemed appropriate to devote an entire issue to what many Alaskans call ANWR (*Anwahr*) and what most of the rest of the nation knows as the Arctic Refuge. For an in-depth look at the land, and its flora, fauna and geological resources, the early explorers, and pioneer conservationist Margaret E. (Mardy) Murie, we called on writer Debbie S. Miller, of Fairbanks, who has explored the refuge for nearly 20 years. For an account of two families who have lived off the resources of the refuge, we turned to Roger Kaye, a free-lance writer and U.S. Fish and Wildlife Service employee out of Fairbanks. For a discussion of Kaktovik and Arctic Village, the two communities closest to the refuge, and the politics surrounding the refuge, we looked to L.J. Campbell, our staff writer.

SUBMITTING PHOTOGRAPHS: Please write for a list of upcoming topics or other specific photo needs and a copy of our editorial guidelines. We cannot be responsible for unsolicited submissions. Submissions not accompanied by sufficient postage for return by certified mail will be returned by regular mail.

CHANGE OF ADDRESS: The post office does not automatically forward *ALASKA GEOGRAPHIC*® when you move. To ensure continuous service, please notify us six weeks before moving. Send your new address, and, if possible, your membership number or a mailing label from a recent *ALASKA GEOGRAPHIC*® to: The Alaska Geographic Society, P.O. Box 93370, Anchorage, AK 99509-3370.

MAILING LISTS: We occasionally make our members' names and addresses available to carefully screened companies and publications whose products and activities may be of interest to you. If you prefer not to receive such mailings, please advise us, and include your mailing label (or your name and address if label is not available).

The Library of Congress has cataloged this serial publication as follows:

Alaska Geographic. v.1-
 [Anchorage, Alaska Geographic Society] 1972-
 v. ill. (part col.). 23 x 31 cm.
 Quarterly
 Official publication of The Alaska Geographic Society.
 Key title: Alaska geographic, ISSN 0361-1353.

 1. Alaska—Description and travel—1959-
 —Periodicals. I. Alaska Geographic Society.

F901.A266 917.98'04'505 72-92087

Library of Congress 75[79112] MARC-S

We acknowledge the assistance of several scientists who provided information for this issue and/or reviewed portions of the text including Gil Mull, of the Alaska Division of Geological and Geophysical Surveys; Tom McCabe and Mark Willms of the U.S. Fish and Wildlife Service's Alaska Fish and Wildlife Research Center in Fairbanks; Robert Lipkin, botanist with the Alaska Natural Heritage Program; Tom Edgerton, outdoor recreation planner, and Donald P. Garrett, acting refuge manager in Fairbanks; and A. Robyn Thorson, associate regional director, and Ann Rappoport, biologist, both with the U.S. Fish and Wildlife Service regional office in Anchorage. For sharing their experiences, we thank Glenn Elison, deputy director of refuges in Alaska, who was ANWR manager from 1983 until early 1993, and Averill Thayer, ANWR's first manager from 1969 through 1981. We appreciate the assistance of Bob Childers of Anchorage and the staff of the Gwich'in Steering Committee for reviewing the Arctic Village text; of Selina Hamilton in the Kaktovik mayor's office for having the article about Kaktovik reviewed; and of the staff of the Alaska Native Language Center for help with the spellings and pronounciation of Inupiat names.

COLOR SEPARATIONS BY: Graphic Chromatics

PRINTED BY: Hart Press

PRINTED IN U.S.A.

COVER: *A backpacker heads south up Itkillik Creek toward Guilbeau Pass to the Chandalar drainage through a field of dwarf fireweed. Itkillik Creek enters the Hulahula River near the river's headwaters in an area known as the big bend. (William Wakeland)*

PREVIOUS PAGE: *Rolling hills and boreal forest typify the southern regions of the Arctic National Wildlife Refuge. (George Matz)*

FACING PAGE: *Dall sheep stand guard on pre-Mississippian (more than 360 million years old) rocks east of the Jago River. (Paige Peapples)*

Contents

Introduction

A female American tree sparrow flushed from her cup-shaped nest in a willow as I trudged through soggy tundra near Grassers, a gravel landing strip for planes depositing passengers near the headwaters of the Hulahula River. I had come to the Arctic National Wildlife Refuge to float the river, and to see a bit of what this famed northeastern Alaska wilderness was all about. I would spend 10 days on the river, floating on the braided stream that gained strength and depth as it flowed north through the Brooks Range. The Hulahula left the mountains in an S-shaped curve of turbulence that demanded skill and concentration from would-be river floaters. Beyond the curve, the Hulahula's channel flattened, gravel bars and cut banks guided the way to deeper water and all were at the mercy of the wind.

Our group put out just upriver from the Hulahula's mouth, with the DEW-line towers of Kaktovik visible in the distance. Bulky Mount Michelson loomed in the other direction, vanguard of a mountain rampart honoring geologist Alfred Hulse Brooks that stretched across the southern horizon. Since leaving the mountains, we had seen grizzlies, caribou, red fox, musk ox, a distant wolf, numerous rodents and a multitude of birds. Most of all, we had experienced a sense of tranquility and expansiveness. Here, man does not dominate.

To acquaint readers with this corner of Alaska, we called on Debbie S. Miller, who has explored this region for 18 years. Currently a resident of Fairbanks, Debbie has taught school in Arctic Village and is the author of *Midnight Wilderness* (1990).

—Penny Rennick, Editor

FACING PAGE: *Porcupine Lake, more than a mile long, lies in the Philip Smith Mountains between the headwaters of the Marsh Fork of the Canning River and the Ivishak River. (Stuart Pechek)*

The Hulahula River carves an S-shaped channel as it leaves the Brooks Range and heads out onto the coastal plain. Mount Chamberlin, its summit partially obscured by clouds, dominates this view of a portion of the Franklin Mountains. (Bill Sherwonit)

Arctic National Wildlife Refuge

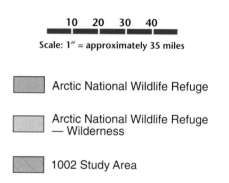

10 20 30 40

Scale: 1" = approximately 35 miles

Arctic National Wildlife Refuge

Arctic National Wildlife Refuge — Wilderness

1002 Study Area

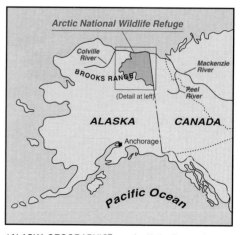

(ALASKA GEOGRAPHIC® map by Kathy Doogan)

TOP LEFT: *River floaters make camp on the banks of the Hulahula River near Old Woman Creek. A hike later in the evening flushed grizzlies hunting on the slopes of the mountain behind camp, and a red fox trotted through camp the next morning. (Penny Rennick)*

LEFT: *The Hulahula River flows north from the Romanzof Mountains about 100 miles to Camden Bay on the arctic coast, in places cutting through meta-sedimentary rocks probably at least 570 million years old. (Bill Sherwonit)*

ABOVE: *Ammerman Mountain (3,000 feet) rises behind this landscape of stunted black spruce covered with 4 to 5 feet of snow along Bilwaddy Creek in the extreme eastern portion of the refuge. (David G. Roseneau)*

FACING PAGE: *Scarlet bearberry brightens a tundra ridge in the Sadlerochit Mountains, looking south toward the Franklin Mountains and Mount Chamberlin, at 9,020 feet the highest point in the Brooks Range. (Scott T. Smith)*

An Arctic Dream

By Debbie S. Miller

At 19.2 million acres, the Arctic National Wildlife Refuge is the nation's largest, nearly the size of the state of Maine. It is one of 16 national refuges in Alaska that were established, or enlarged, under the 1980 Alaska National Interest Lands Conservation Act. In summary, the Arctic Refuge was created with four purposes: to conserve fish and wildlife populations and their habitats in their natural diversity; to fulfill international treaty obligations, such as migratory waterfowl agreements and the Canada-United States Porcupine caribou herd agreement; to provide an opportunity for local residents to continue their subsistence way of life; and to protect water quality and its quantity within the refuge.

The Arctic Refuge is divided into three distinct physiographic regions. In the north lies the arctic coastal plain, calving grounds for the 163,000-member Porcupine caribou herd, and home to many migratory and resident bird species. South of the coastal plain the Brooks Range forms the largest region within the refuge. These mountains, which include the highest peaks in the range, arc gently east to west across the refuge, stretching for more than 200 miles. South of the mountains lies a rolling landscape of boreal forest, with numerous lakes, rivers and streams. Each region provides important habitat for a diversity of flora and fauna.

Now let's go explore the Arctic Refuge.

FACING PAGE: *Musk oxen are the only large mammals active year-round on the coastal plain. Although musk oxen are highly social and usually found in mixed-sex groups, these bachelor bulls gathered along the Canning River in June. Musk oxen were exterminated from the North Slope in the late-1800s, but 64 were reintroduced to the coastal plain in 1969 and 1970. The 35 surviving animals multiplied exponentially and now about 550 musk oxen live on the North Slope, with about 350 of them on the refuge's coastal plain. (Marta McWhorter)*

The Coastal Plain

We paddle down the Canning River into a fierce northeast wind. Some of the gusts force us upstream. I hunker down in the kayak with my legs draped over the front of the boat, my seat forward and my back slumped down. Less wind resistance, but like a water beetle on its back, not the best position for paddling.

Crossing the coastal plain at a snail's pace, we hope for the momentary wind shelter of a cut bank, bluff or a rising slope in the distance. On the open plain there is little to break the might of wind. Scrubby willows screen the wind along the rivers, but they don't stop it. Pingos, those circular mounds of earth thrust upwards by permafrost, provide little relief. The wind just circles the pingo and finds us anyway, like a river rounding a boulder in its path.

We stroke into the wall of wind for 15 miles. Our greatest challenge is cutting our paddles through the wind without having them blown from our hands. Northeast winds prevail along the arctic coast most of the year. During summer, gale force winds on the coastal plain can blow more than 40 mph. Winter winds have been clocked as high as 90 plus mph at Barter Island, with wind chill factors dipping well below minus 100. Calm days are few.

The 125-mile-long Canning River forms part of the western boundary of the Arctic Refuge. This river, born in the Philip Smith Mountains, is the longest of the refuge's 14 major rivers that flow north out of the Brooks Range and cross the coastal plain to the Beaufort Sea. Explorer Sir John Franklin named the river during his 1826 expedition along the arctic coast in honor of George Canning, later the British Prime Minister.

The Canning is one of the few rivers that has acquired an English name. Most of the rivers have Inupiat Eskimo names that usually reflect physical characteristics of the particular river: the Katakturak (*KutukTOOruck*), "river where you can see a long way"; the

Caribou trails mark this patch of tundra along Camden Bay. The geometrical patterns in the tundra result from freezing and thawing of water. (Pamela A. Miller)

RIGHT: Arctophyla fulva, *a grass, grows around lakeshores, along streams and in shallow water on the coastal plain. Snow geese eat this species in spring. (Una Swain)*

LOWER RIGHT: *A short-tailed weasel pauses near a rock on the Jago River delta. In winter, its fur turns white except the tip of its tail, which remains black. Also known as the ermine, the short-tailed weasel feeds on lemmings, birds, eggs, young hares, insects and fish. (Pamela A. Miller)*

Iqalugliurak (*EekaloogLEUruck*), "little creek with lots of fish"; the Okpilak (*OokPEEluck*), "river with no willows"; the Kongakut (*KONGakut*), "farthest away river." With place names, white explorers often honored people, while Inupiat honored place, based on their strong ties to the land.

As we paddle closer to the Canning River delta, the wind increases, and our cheeks feel the icy cold of the pack ice that rims the coast. My husband, Dennis, spots a gravel bar that looks like a possible landing site for our pilot, who is scheduled to pick us up the next day. We pull our boat out of the water, and camp in the lee of an old river cut bank.

The river terrace is covered with dryas, a member of the rose family with dainty, eight-petaled, white flowers. Dryas grows a few inches above the ground on supple stems that flex with the strongest of gales. In today's wind, the flower heads bend to the ground, lacing the lichens and mosses that grow around them. The prolific dryas, scattered across the coastal plain, is eaten by caribou.

We groom the gravel bar, removing any large boulders that might cause a problem for a small plane. The strip, shaped like a half-eaten banana, is our connection to civilization. For the past month we have trekked through the Brooks Range between the Hulahula and Canning rivers, hiked the Marsh Fork of the Canning and then floated the river's lower part across a 40-mile stretch of coastal plain. In all this time we have not seen another human, only the occasional passing plane.

I toss a few rocks, then stop to look at a patch of yellow oxytropis

that brightens the bleached river stones. Through the howl of wind there's a change in the steady flow of river, a muffled thrashing of water. Not far from us a cow moose splashes across the river. With no trees to dwarf her, she looks huge on the flat sweep of tundra. As she exits the water on to the gravel bar, the long dewclaws above her hooves appear, and it looks as though she is wearing high heels on the bar.

She heads off across the tundra, like a striking dark horse on this northernmost meadow. In the many years that we have explored the coastal plain, we have only occasionally seen moose so near the Beaufort Sea. The majority of moose are scattered in the foothills and mountain valleys where they browse mainly on willows. But a few wander out to the coast, to the final fringe of tundra.

Maroon and green shale bluffs hem the Clarence River, which begins and ends in Yukon Territory but flows through the Arctic Refuge for several miles south of Demarcation Point in the extreme northeastern corner of Alaska. Sir John Franklin named the river for a member of the British royalty. (Arne Bakke)

Late in the day, the wind calms as the sun makes its gradual arc toward the Beaufort Sea. For our month of wilderness travel we were without watches in the 24-hour daylight. We had learned to gauge time by the position of the sun. When it dropped to its lowest point above the northern horizon, and the sky turned a brilliant salmon, it was midnight. When the sun reached its zenith to the south, it was lunch time, or on some days, breakfast time. Here, the sun remains above the horizon between May 15 and July 27.

With the wind silenced, the croaking of ptarmigan, lilting of Lapland longspurs and peeping of sandpipers enliven the tundra. In a nearby pond a pair of red-necked phalaropes pirouette on the water, stirring up the sediments for insect larvae. Their heads bob persistently, their bills needle the pond like a sewing machine.

Each summer, hundreds of thousands of birds migrate to the coastal plain to breed and feed. About 135 bird species have been recorded on this rolling plain of tundra that stretches east 140 miles to the Canadian border. Sandwiched between the Brooks Range and the Beaufort Sea, the coastal plain offers ideal nesting habitat with its wetlands, upland tussock slopes and riparian environments. Many of the migratory species thrive on insects, and birds such as pectoral and buff-breasted sandpipers time the hatching of their chicks to the explosion of insect life in June and July.

This distant arctic plain and its food supply are so attractive that species such as red-necked phalarope, semipalmated sandpiper and lesser golden plover travel thousands of miles each year to nest here. As summer wanes, the phalaropes will migrate to waters off the coast of Mexico and South America, the semipalmated sandpipers to Venezuela and the plovers to the pampas of central South America. [**Editor's note:** *In fall 1993, the American Ornithologists Union is expected to announce the splitting of the lesser golden plover species into two distinct species, American golden plover and Pacific golden plover. American golden plovers are the ones breeding on the Arctic Refuge.*]

On top of a nearby pingo are some owl pellets and a few scattered feathers. Inside the hairy pellet are small teeth and bones of a vole or lemming, the main prey of owls. The snowy owl with its thick, white plumage and 5-foot wingspan, is one of six non-migratory bird species on the coastal plain. Others include raven; rock and willow ptarmigan; gyrfalcon, which feed primarily on ptarmigan; and dipper, found locally near year-round warm springs.

From the pingo, the vastness of the landscape unfolds. To the east my eyes drift across the lowlands, the marshy tundra with its duck-specked ponds and ice-wedge polygons giving the plain a rice-paddy appearance. Beyond, my eyes see an endless, undulating slope of tussocks, with no obstructions to mask the landform. It is an open, free-roaming wilderness bordered on the south by the Brooks Range. The vista from the coast to the mountains frees the eye and unclutters the mind.

Most of the coastal plain is classified as wetlands because permafrost usually keeps the water table at or near the surface. The 1- to 2-foot active layer of permafrost, where annual thawing occurs,

This newborn caribou calf blends into its bed of grasses and sedges near the Okpilak River on the coastal plain. The vegetation provides camouflage for the calves from predators such as wolves, eagles and bears. Caribou calves are able to stand and nurse within an hour after birth, and are capable of traveling with adults within a week. (Stuart Pechek)

In early June, a biologist scans still-brown cottongrass near Sadler-ochit Spring, part of the tussock-covered coastal plain uplands used by calving caribou. The spring, fed by warm water in the 50-degree range year-round, is the only location known north of the Brooks Range for several plant species. In the distance to the south, Kikiktat Mountain (5,000 feet) appears just above the large snow patch. To the left is Mount Michelson (8,855 feet), and Mount Chamberlin (9,020 feet) can be seen at the extreme right. (David G. Roseneau)

is saturated with snowmelt during the brief arctic summer. Except for Sadlerochit Spring with its year-round flow, the rest of the coastal plain is thought to be underlain by permafrost, with depths ranging from 1,000 to 2,000 feet.

Conversely, these wetlands receive little precipitation. The coastal plain receives about as much moisture as the Mojave Desert, about 6 inches annually. Yet, drainage is limited due to the permafrost, and the evaporation rate is low. What little rain soaks into the tundra remains.

To the north, where waves of the Beaufort lap the ragged edge of tundra, are the coastal lagoons, then an endless table of sea ice stretching to the North Pole. This icescape is home to polar bear, and ringed and bearded seals. In summer and fall, bowhead and beluga whales migrate through leads in offshore ice. The bowheads, seals, and fish such as arctic char and arctic cisco, are an important food source for some 225 Inupiat villagers of Kaktovik.

The river deltas, lagoons and coastal waters offer excellent habitat for a variety of waterfowl and 62 species of marine and anadromous fish. Several hundred tundra swans, and smaller populations of

Canada geese, greater white-fronted geese and lesser snow geese have been known to breed near the refuge's major deltas. As many as 33 species of waterfowl feed, molt and stage prior to migration on coastal lagoons, barrier islands and sand spits. The most abundant are oldsquaw ducks with lesser numbers of common and king eiders; black, white-winged and surf scoters; red-throated, Pacific and yellow-billed loons; red and red-necked phalaropes; arctic terns; glaucous, Thayer's, herring and sabine's gulls; and long-tailed, parasitic and pomarine jaegers. Government reports for the last three years do not list sightings of spectacled eiders, but Native hunters have brought in carcasses, an indication that this threatened species also uses the coastal waters.

The coastal plain is a relatively small region within the Arctic Refuge, about 2 million acres or 10 percent of the refuge. Yet, this rich swath of plain, averaging 25 to 30 miles wide, offers habitat for the greatest concentrations and diversity of wildlife in the entire refuge.

The plain is a wildlife mecca. In late May and early June as many as 70,000 to 80,000 female caribou of the Porcupine herd migrate here to deliver their calves and feed on summer plant growth. Later in June the remainder of the herd, approximately 90,000 animals, arrives on the coastal plain. When the caribou arrive, snow still mottles the plain, and the caribou graze on early budding cotton-grass. As the snow disappears, the caribou feed on a succession of vitamin-rich plants needed after their winter diet of lichens.

In early June, usually during a two-day period, calving peaks, although the first calving begins in late May and the last concludes about mid-June. As many as 40,000 calves are born each year. At the same time, thousands of migratory birds are arriving. Each species establishes its territory, be it near a pond, in the tussocks, on a gravel bar or in willow thickets along a river. Courtship rituals

A pair of hikers explores the coastal plain along the Okpilak River, which starts at the Okpilak Glacier in the Romanzof Mountains and runs north 70 miles to Camden Bay. (Dennis and Debbie Miller)

and bird songs warm the arctic air. Well-camouflaged nests are built once again. As countless nests are completed, arctic foxes can be often seen prowling for eggs. During summer months, these foxes feed largely on rodents, eggs and chicks, and they often cache their prey for later use. Both arctic and red foxes inhabit the coastal plain, although arctic foxes predominate. Kaktovik residents trap foxes in the winter for their fur.

In late June and early July, when temperatures sometimes soar into the 70s and 80s, the caribou aggregate by the tens of

thousands, brought together by harassing mosquitoes and other insects. Giant herds move across the tundra to the rhythm of grunts and snorts, mooing and bleating and the unique clicking of the caribou's hooves.

As the caribou mass together, birds are hatching amid a profusion of wildflowers. Peeping sandpipers peck at insects. Adult Lapland longspurs, one of the most abundant passerines on the coastal plain, busily feed their nestlings. Common and hoary redpolls nurture chicks hidden in cup-shaped nests near willow thickets. Semipalmated plovers scurry along gravel bars.

As temperatures rise in mid- to late June on the coastal plain, swarms of mosquitoes emerge. On warm, calm days these biting insects drive the caribou into breezes along the coast on barrier islands, shallows of lagoons, gravel bars, or into the mountains. This group found relief on ice floes at land's edge. (Dennis and Debbie Miller)

By September, most of the caribou and smaller birds have left the coastal plain, but not the geese and ducks. From late August through mid-September as many as 325,000 lesser snow geese arrive on the plain to rest and feed before migrating south. Greater white-fronted geese and smaller black brant also stage in fall on the plain and its fringe of salt marshes.

As autumn snows cover the coastal plain, the last of the waterfowl migrate. Though many species have departed, year-round residents remain. A re-established musk ox herd, scattered in small groups in several river drainages, now numbers about 350 on the refuge. Wolves, arctic foxes, wolverines, arctic ground squirrels and small rodents prepare for winter. Grizzlies have left the coastal plain for the foothills and mountains, where they continue looking for food until time to den.

Although many female polar bears spend the winter in offshore ice caves, studies show that the coastal plain has the highest concentration of land-denning polar bears on Alaska's North Slope. In October, pregnant females seek out den sites along riverbanks and on the leeward side of bluffs where sufficient snow has accumulated. Most bears den along the coast, although they have denned up to 32 miles inland.

In December or January, one or two cubs are born in snow caves. Mothers and cubs emerge from their dens in spring, and soon head to sea on the drifting pack ice in search of ringed seals, their main prey. The Beaufort Sea polar bear population numbers about 2,000.

Back on the Canning, Dennis has caught an arctic char for dinner. We sit near the water, watching midnight sun colors, listening to the gentle flow of a braided river. We camp on a major dividing line. To the west lies the land open to oil and gas development. Prudhoe Bay, with its web of roads, pipelines and drilling pads, is only 65 miles away. To the east, the coastal plain of the Arctic Refuge is the only stretch of North Slope coastline protected within a conservation unit in the United States.

After years of biological studies, oil and gas assessments and political debates, it remains uncertain whether the coastal plain will stay wilderness or be opened to industrial development.

The Mountains

The tranquil flow of the Hulahula River grows more distant as we gain elevation above the valley floor. Tundra slopes, in their peak of summer greenery, gently rise from the river. The rolling, treeless slopes of this broad, U-shaped valley grace the highest mountains in the Brooks Range, the Romanzofs.

We hike up the tussock-matted slope toward Mount Michelson, northernmost prominent mountain of these glacier-capped peaks. Dennis and I, and our friend Jim Swanson, hope to reach Michelson's summit, at 8,855 feet the third highest in this mountain group. When compared to other mountains, the Romanzofs are not particularly high, yet the dramatic rise from the 2,000-foot level of the river basins to the 8,000- to 9,000-foot mountain summits is impressive.

Mountains of the northeastern Brooks Range formed relatively recently in geologic time, about 300 to 350 million years ago. In

These hikers do some ridge walking in the Romanzof Mountains on the north side of the Kongakut River. This view is looking southwestward. (William Wakeland)

ABOVE: *This adult, male hoary marmot shows the colorful markings characteristic of the Brooks Range subspecies found scattered throughout the refuge in the Romanzof, Franklin and Philip Smith mountains. The buffy reddish-orange pelage and black and white stripes are most pronounced in the males. (David G. Roseneau)*

TOP RIGHT: *These four young gray-phase gyrfalcons (one is lying down behind another) will soon be mature enough to fly from their nest along tree line in the Brooks Range. Gyrfalcons are found year-round in the Arctic Refuge. Two subspecies of peregrine falcon also inhabit the refuge: the arctic subspecies, listed as threatened under the Endangered Species Act, lives on the coastal plain and in the mountains. The endangered American subspecies lives on the south side, where some individuals nest along the bluffs above the Porcupine River. (David G. Roseneau)*

the past the granite core that is now the heart of the Romanzofs underlay a shallow sea bed with live corals and other sea life, skeletons of which have fossilized and can now be found scattered along the riverbeds. In theory, this one-time mountainless region lay submerged near the edge of the North American continent, as part of the North Pacific plate. This land had not yet merged with the Arctic-Alaska plate.

Geologists speculate that things changed dramatically about 135 to 150 million years ago. The North Pacific plate collided with the more stationary Arctic-Alaska plate. Gradually the Brooks Range from about the present-day Dalton Highway west, was squeezed upward by tectonic pressure. A sedimentary marine basin remained

This rock glacier in the Sadlerochit Mountains may flow slowly like an ice glacier. Such rock glaciers are thought to be laced with ice in the spaces between the rocks. (Gil Mull)

to the northeast. About 60 million years ago, the northeastern Brooks Range began to rise from this basin.

The Romanzofs, in turn, were uplifted to become mountains in the Brooks Range. More interesting to geologists is the fact that the Romanzofs and neighboring Sadlerochits are relatively young compared with the rest of the Brooks Range. Geologic signs indicate uplift has occurred during the last few million years. Past and recent mountain-building events, known as "thermal pulses," have exposed more than a billion years of old and new rocks.

Old formations include 800-million-year-old Katakturak dolomite in the Sadlerochit Mountains; and 300-million-year-old limestone of the Lisburne formation, a layer averaging about 2,000 feet thick and exposed in many areas throughout the Brooks Range. Erosion by rivers, snow, ice and wind has weathered the limestone into striking crags, cliffs, ridges and canyons.

Younger deposits include 65,000 to 70,000-year-old sandstone and shale along the Canning River, and moraines left by receding glaciers during the Pleistocene glaciation that ended about 10,000 years ago.

Exposed sedimentary and metamorphic formations have often been thrusted, folded and fractured from the many episodes of uplifting. It's not uncommon to see walls of rock tilted on their sides or strata that have been compressed and folded into hairpin turns. For the geologist, the northeastern Brooks Range is a museum of rock, with formations from every geologic period visible.

Dennis, Jim and I continue up the slope, passing patches of white heather, pink bistort and clumps of Alaska boykinia, generally known as bear flower. A member of the saxifrage family, this plant grows to 3 feet in height; and grizzlies, which feed on its flowers, leaves and roots, are commonly seen in this region. We scan the slope frequently for bears.

The headwaters of Cane Creek are here, at the Continental Divide in the Philip Smith Mountains. Cane Creek flows 22 miles southeast to the East Fork Chandalar River. The valley offers good alpine tundra walking, with access across the divide into the upper Canning River drainage. (Dennis Miller)

About 800 grizzlies inhabit the Arctic Refuge, most of them in the Brooks Range. Unlike in southern Alaska where brown bears congregate to feed on salmon, arctic grizzlies are not considered fish-eaters. They lead more solitary lives, require larger individual territories — home ranges average 500 to 600 square miles for adult males — and feed on a varied diet of plants, roots, berries, arctic ground squirrels, caribou and other mammals.

Soon we reach a layer of fog that hems us from above. I pause to take one last look at the braided Hulahula River before we lose visibility. This glacier-fed river, named by Hawaiian whalers in the 1890s, flows north through the mountains for about 40 miles, carving a silver path through centuries of gravel deposits and old glacial till. Fed by numerous tributaries and shouldered by tundra slopes, it rumbles through an S-shaped gorge onto the expansive coastal plain, running another 40 miles to the Beaufort Sea. Kaktovik residents traditionally hunt and fish along its channel.

When geologist Ernest Leffingwell explored the Hulahula River between 1906 and 1914, he calculated that a glacier as much as 1,500 feet thick once gripped the valley from the continental divide at the Brooks Range crest to its terminus just north of the mountains.

Because of the river's spectacular scenery and diversity of wildlife, it is one of the most popular recreational rivers. Each June and July commercial guides and visitors float the Hulahula and other north-flowing streams such as the Canning, Aichilik and Kongakut. The visitors come to experience the unsurpassed wilderness and wildlife diversity of the Arctic Refuge, which has only the two communities, Kaktovik and Arctic Village, along its borders. In fact, the refuge coupled with its neighbor in northwestern Yukon Territory, Ivvavik (formerly Northern Yukon) National Park, comprises one of the largest and most isolated protected block of wild habitat in North America. No other conservation unit protects such a wide spectrum of arctic and subarctic species.

The black, grizzly and polar bear are all here. Caribou, musk ox, moose, Dall sheep, wolf, fox, wolverine, beaver and muskrat, marten and otter, arctic ground squirrel and porcupine, lynx and snowshoe hare, voles and lemmings are here.

All totaled, the refuge supports 169 species of birds, 38 species of fish, 44 species of mammals, an unknown number of species of insects, about 600 species of flowering plants and more than 2,000 species of lichens and bryophytes (mosses and liverworts). When compared with latitudes closer to the equator, the number of species is low. Costa Rica, for example, is roughly two-thirds the size of the Arctic Refuge, and hosts 500,000 species of tropical plants and animals.

But numbers alone do not reflect the value of habitat. Although the Arctic and Subarctic have fewer species, these species are adapted to one of the harshest climates on earth, and most of these circumpolar species are not found in temperate and tropical regions. Scientists have yet to complete an inventory of insect species in Alaska, and relatively little is known about how arctic and subarctic species of plants and insects might benefit humans.

Dennis, Jim and I climb several hundred feet through a thick layer of fog, with restricted visibility. At one point, a bull caribou with velvet-covered antlers appears for a moment like an apparition, then vanishes into the mist. After gaining about 2,500 feet, we begin to break out of the fog. For the first time, we see the massive white shoulder of Mount Michelson rising behind a thin veil of glittering mist.

At our base camp on a moraine beneath Mount Michelson, the panoramic view is magical. Like islands, the surrounding mountains loom above a sea of fog. To the west, on the other side of the Hulahula, Mount Chamberlin rises dramatically to 9,020 feet, the highest peak in the Brooks Range. When John Milton and Kenneth Brower first saw Chamberlin, Milton described the mountain as "a nearly perfect cone of rock and snow," and "the most beautiful peak" that he had seen on their month-long trek through the mountains in 1967. Chamberlin, indeed, dominates the western horizon, towering above the 5,000- to 7,000-foot-high Franklin Mountains.

Hidden in the fog beneath Chamberlin are the two largest lakes in the refuge, Schrader and Peters. The lakes were named for geologists Frank Charles Schrader (1860-1944) and William John Peters (1863-1942) who, in the early 1900s, explored and mapped

TOP RIGHT: *The Aichilik River flows north out of the Romanzof Mountains through this cleft in the rocks, and across the coastal plain to Beaufort Lagoon. (Pamela A. Miller)*

RIGHT: *Flowering plants grow tenaciously in the rocky soils of the refuge's mountains. Among them is the arctic sandwort, a low-growing, white-petaled perennial found in arctic and alpine tundra and heathlands. These sandworts are found throughout much of Alaska and western and northern Yukon Territory in Canada. (Gil Mull)*

A lone wolf pauses in June's midnight sun at 12:30 a.m. on the rock moraine of Esetuk Glacier, on Mount Michelson's flank above the Hulahula River. Wolves use drainage systems such as this as travel corridors in their wide-ranging quest for caribou, moose, sheep, ground squirrels, rodents and birds. Five packs of wolves with about 30 members total live in the refuge on the north side of the Brooks Range. Wolf population estimates for the refuge's south side are not available. (Karen Jettmar)

mountains, northernmost in the country, are young and still growing. Strangely, one of the oldest pre-Cambrian rock formations of the refuge, Katakturak dolomite, is exposed in the youngest mountains of the refuge.

The Shubliks and Sadlerochits are known for their year-round flowing springs. Shublik Spring originates on the western end of the Shubliks near Cache Creek. This spring nourishes lush vegetation that supports bird species well north of their normal distribution. An isolated stand of balsam poplar provides habitat for nesting robins, gray jays and yellow-shafted flickers. Moose browse on the poplars and willows in spring. Grizzlies, caribou, wolverines and wolves also commonly use the area.

Sadlerochit Spring, on the east end of the Sadlerochit Mountains, is one of the largest perennial springs on the North Slope, and provides wintering areas for arctic char and arctic grayling. Some ferns, sedges and avens species are found nowhere else so far north. Both springs are among 39 sites in the Brooks Range that have been nominated as National Natural Landmarks.

Behind our tent, Esetuk Glacier crawls down the slopes of Mount Michelson for five miles, with part of its glacial field heavily crevassed. With a clear view of the west face of Michelson, we study our proposed climbing route, and sort out gear for the next day's planned ascent.

While scanning beyond the glacier, we spot a dozen Dall sheep grazing on tundra ridges below us. The upper slopes of the Hulahula and other north-flowing rivers in the refuge provide excellent sheep habitat. Of the estimated 30,000 Dall sheep in the

the Brooks Range and arctic coast. The Inupiat, who continue to subsist off the resources in this region, refer to the lakes as Nervokpuk (*NarVUCKpuck*), or "big lake."

These two glacier-fed lakes are connected by an inlet, and stretch for about nine miles through the northern edge of the Franklin Mountains. Like wings of the golden eagle, these long, deep bodies of water cut through the mountains, mirroring the backdrop of peaks and ridges. They offer productive habitat for lake trout, arctic grayling and arctic char, and Kaktovik residents traditionally come here by snow machine in spring to ice fish for lake trout.

Schrader and Peters lakes are also where in summer 1952 scientists A. Starker Leopold and Frank Fraser Darling camped with National Park Service surveyors George Collins and Lowell Sumner. Here they discussed the idea of protecting this region as a wilderness park or refuge. Collins thought that the region was "the finest national park prospect that he had ever seen," because of the high mountains, range of habitats and diversity of wildlife.

To the northwest rise the 4,000- to 5,000-foot tops of the Shublik and Sadlerochit mountains. Geologists think that these

Brooks Range, about one-third live in the Arctic Refuge. The majority of these prefer drainages on the north side of the range because northern valleys receive less annual snowfall than those on the south side and valleys with low-lying passes, such as the Hulahula, Canning and Kongakut, are scoured by strong winds, which expose vegetation important for the sheep's winter diet.

Above the sheep, a golden eagle soars overhead on its 6-foot wingspan. One of 19 raptor species identified in the Arctic Refuge, golden eagles, and other birds of prey such as gyrfalcons and rough-legged hawks, nest in the mountains and foothills.

A variety of passerines and shorebirds migrate to the refuge's mountain valleys to breed. Northern wheatears come from as far away as Africa. Arctic warblers journey from southern Asia. Wandering tattlers fly in from Hawaii. The fact that adult birds make these phenomenal annual migrations is impressive, but it seems miraculous that their offspring are capable of flying such great distances in their first months of life.

We awaken to a blue sky, crisp temperatures, light air and a fogless world. The climbing conditions are ideal. We strap on our crampons, rope up and cross Esetuk Glacier. After snaking our way around a field of crevasses, we climb up the shoulder of Mount Michelson on a glittering snowfield with the sun baking us.

With 1,000 feet to go, we reach a 45-degree, ice-covered cone in line with the summit. Below this section of sheer ice is a 2,000-foot drop to the glacier. The exposure is awesome. Although we are using ice axes and crampons, it would be impossible to sustain a self-arrest if one person fell. A fall would mean the unthinkable, a great slide down an ice chute that we'd never remember.

Dennis and I went first. Never before have I so carefully planned, concentrated and executed each step, jabbing the precious points of my crampons into the wall of ice, piercing the slope with my ice axes, like a fork into an ice cube. The crampons grabbed to life, not just ice. One slip, one mistake, and we were both goners. We never looked down the slope, only at our feet. After 800 feet of steady ice climbing, we reached the summit ridge with great relief. Dennis descended to accompany Jim up the slope. I stood alone, in the greatest silence I've ever experienced, absorbing the entire Brooks Range for as far as my eye could see.

This day on the summit there's not a trace of wind. There is a forever vista: mountains upon mountains, valleys and more valleys,

Esetuk Glacier reaches down the northeast slope of Mount Michelson in the Romanzof Mountains. (Gil Mull)

most of them nameless, many of the peaks unclimbed. About 200 miles of the 600-mile-long Brooks Range lie within the Arctic Refuge. This rampart of mountains stretches south for about 100 miles. Around me lay a magnificent 20,000 square miles of mountains with only a few human settlements on the southern fringe. One can arguably state that this range comprises the wildest mountainous region remaining in North America.

From this vantage point seven distinct mountain provinces can be seen. Toward the Canadian border lie the distant British and Davidson mountains. The mountains drop off near the border, with the Continental Divide measuring just 2,000 feet. In the low-lying Davidson Mountains, north-flowing Firth River and Mancha Creek support the only stands of white and black spruce on the north side of the Brooks Range.

Turning clockwise, the Romanzofs encircle us, then the Franklin Mountains. Serrated ridge crests of the distant Philip Smith Mountains lie to the west and south; the Sadlerochit and Shublik mountains rise to the northwest.

To the north, the mountains give way to the foothills, and we can see where glaciers once pushed onto the southern edge of the

BELOW: *Mount Michelson, at 8,855-feet, dominates the skyline as seen from lower elevations in the Romanzof Mountains to the north. (Gil Mull)*

RIGHT: *Debbie Miller stands at the summit of Mount Michelson after careful ascent of a 45-degree sheer ice wall some 1,000 feet below. The refuge's coastal plain to the north can been seen in the background. (Dennis Miller)*

coastal plain. Lateral moraines, now covered with a thin layer of tundra, front the mountains for 10 or more miles. These waves of glacial till were left in the wake of ice. A few glacial lakes, such as Okpilak, glisten far below, remnants of the receding ice. Six glaciations during the Pleistocene and Holocene (more than 2 million years ago to present time) once carved all of these surrounding valleys. Today, the only large active glacier system remaining in the Brooks Range is here in the Romanzof Mountains.

Beyond the foothills, I can see the sweep of coastal plain rolling north to the Beaufort Sea, then a table of sea ice curving toward the North Pole. Never before have I felt such freedom of space, such quiet and solitude, such wildness.

Back at our base camp, with sore ankles and knees, we were thankful for what the mountains had given us. We would later find out that the first recorded ascent of Mount Michelson was made in April 1957 by John Thomson, a writer with the Fairbanks *Daily News-Miner*, and Reynold E. (Pete) Isto (1913-1965), a U.S. Geological Survey engineer, for whom Mount Isto (8,975 feet) was later named. We learned that they followed our same climbing route but with much greater hardship. Thomson froze his feet on the ascent and was unable to wear regular footgear on the eight-mile trek back to the Hulahula River. Instead, he wore crude mukluks made from woolen socks and underwear and the outer cover of a canvas poncho.

Our summit day ended with a spectacular rise of a full moon. From my journal:

August 16. *Just before crawling into the tent, the giant white sphere moved across the southwest horizon. A full moon rose, illuminating the route we had just climbed. I could scarcely sleep. Walking out to the ridge alone, I gazed into the vastness of our 360-degree vista. Mountains upon mountains. Never before had I camped in the Brooks Range high country with such a view. A blanket of orange-tinted fog stretched far to the Beaufort Sea. Esetuk Creek held the only distant sound of rushing water. Teary eyed and chilled, I finally strolled back to the tent, unable to grasp the moment any longer, but the memory was indelible. It was the most beautiful moonrise and day's end I had ever dreamed.*

Autumn colors the tundra around a caribou antler, on the north slope of the Sadlerochit Mountains. (Scott T. Smith)

The South Side

Outside the cabin, a squirrel chatters loudly, announcing a visitor or intruder. I walk into the spruce forest to see what the racket is about, guessing that it might be a marten or a weasel. Scanning from the hummocky forest floor to the crowns of the white spruce, I am stunned. A northern goshawk is perched above me, within 20 to 30 feet and within striking range of the squirrel.

An American dipper attempts to catch grayling fry in the outlet to Old John Lake in early March. Dippers overwinter at groundwater springs and downstream of them in open tunnels in aufeis in some north and south slope drainages in the eastern Brooks Range such as the Ivishak and Canning rivers and Sheenjek and Coleen rivers. (David G. Roseneau)

Piercing red eyes meet blue ones for a few moments, then huge wings whoosh over my head as it flies among the tree tops briefly, then soars off. The squirrel continues its chattering, and my heart still pounds.

I was surprised to see the woodland hawk, especially because it was near the northern edge of its range on the south slope of the Brooks Range. Our home at the time of this bird sighting was a small cabin located near the edge of the mountains on a nameless lake near the Wind River. This site is now part of the 10.3-million-acre southern addition of the Arctic Refuge, established under the Alaska National Interest Lands Conservation Act of 1980.

This addition is bordered on the west by Atigun Pass on the Dalton Highway, on the south by Venetie-Arctic Village tribal lands and Yukon Flats National Wildlife Refuge, and on the east by Canada. Much of this expansion includes the Philip Smith Mountains, birthplace of numerous north- and south-flowing rivers such as the Wind.

Our home was 30 miles south of the northern limit of the spruce forest. Our nearest neighbors were 30 miles northeast in Arctic Village, a Gwich'in Athabaskan Indian village of about 200 people. This community, where English is a second language, borders the Arctic Refuge on the East Fork Chandalar River. The Gwich'in and their ancestors have used the resources of the Arctic Refuge and their tribal lands for thousands of years.

A short distance from our cabin flows the clear waters of the Wind River, a major tributary of the East Fork Chandalar, the largest south-flowing river within the Arctic Refuge. Countless streams drain this watershed, their waters eventually emptying into the Yukon River.

Other major watersheds on the south side include the Sheenjek and Coleen to the east. Portions of the Sheenjek, Wind and north-flowing Ivishak were designated part of the National Wild and Scenic River system in 1980. Of these, the Sheenjek (*Shiinjik* meaning "salmon river" to the Gwich'in) is one of the most popular for floating because of its accessibility and spectacular scenery and wildlife.

The smaller Old Crow River originates in the Davidson

Mountains in the extreme east of the refuge. For most of its length, the Old Crow meanders through Old Crow Flats in Yukon Territory, yet like the Sheenjek and Coleen, the Old Crow merges with the Porcupine River, historical gateway to the Yukon River

Dennis and Debbie Miller built this cabin near the Wind River after Debbie finished teaching at Arctic Village. They lived here during the fall and early winter for three years. (Dennis Miller)

The Junjik River drains a basin west of Arctic Village, flowing out of the Philip Smith Mountains for 65 miles to the East Fork Chandalar River. (George Wuerthner)

for early explorers, traders and miners. High cliffs known as ramparts border a portion of the upper Porcupine that is located within the Arctic Refuge. These colorful gorges intrigue people floating the river, and provide ideal nesting sites for golden eagles and the endangered American subspecies of the peregrine falcon.

While the south side has fewer major rivers, their drainages are much larger. Huge glaciers once scoured the region, leaving spectacular U-shaped valleys. The floor of the valley of the East Fork Chandalar measures 3 to 5 miles wide in many places with valley walls rising 3,000 feet above the river. The rivers offer spawning habitat for chum and king salmon, and a year-round home for arctic grayling, northern pike, burbot and several species of whitefish.

Near the edge of the mountains, the Chandalar, Sheenjek and Wind river valleys are speckled with kettle lakes, many of which also support fish. Old John Lake, one of the largest on the south side, provides abundant habitat for lake trout. Countless smaller lakes support many duck species such as greater and lesser scaups, pintails, oldsquaw, white-winged scoters and buffleheads, and furbearers such as muskrat and beaver.

Long ago the nomadic Gwich'in discovered the abundant resources surrounding Arctic Village. Fish, furbearers, waterfowl, ptarmigan, caribou, moose, Dall sheep, porcupine and timber could all be harvested. Today's residents of Arctic Village rely on these same resources even though the means of harvesting have changed from skin boats to motorized riverboats, dog teams to snow machines, spears to rifles and fish traps to nets.

Back near the Wind River, I stroll to the lake to watch a beaver pushing a cluster of willow branches toward its feed pile. It is late August, and a family of beavers has been busy gathering food for the winter. Beavers are spotty in this area, near the northern limit of their range.

Beyond the beaver's wake, a red-throated loon dives for fish, and scaups paddle near the opposite shore. Four species of loons — common, Pacific, yellow-billed and red-throated — breed in the Arctic Refuge. These ancient residents of earth, among the earliest of bird species to evolve, can be found along the arctic coast, and on lakes in the mountains and on the south side of the Brooks Range. The red-throated loon is striking with its deep red throat, and white and black pinstripes extending up the back of its neck to its crown. Soon this loon will migrate south, wintering along the U.S. west coast or in Baja, Mexico.

Later, Dennis and I walk through the spruce forest and spot a number of forest birds. A three-toed woodpecker pecks for insects in an old spruce. White-winged crossbills gather on the spruces' crowns, scraping seeds out of cones with their cross-tipped bills, perfectly adapted to tearing apart spruce cones. In lower branches, redpolls probe for seeds in the shredded cones the crossbills have dropped. Nearby, a tree squirrel harvests the same cones, heaving them to the ground like a child throwing stones from a mountaintop.

On the south slope of the Brooks Range, the boreal forest and riparian environment attract a diversity of breeding passerines. Based on their 1956 field studies with Olaus and Margaret Murie and Robert Krear, Brina Kessel, a University of Alaska Fairbanks zoology professor, and graduate student George Schaller published *Birds of the Upper Sheenjek Valley, Northeastern Alaska* (1960) in which they list 86 species, many of which were found in the spruce forests and willow thickets.

Forest birds commonly seen during summer and early fall include bohemian waxwings, boreal chickadees, robins, varied and gray-cheeked thrushes, pine grosbeaks, white-winged crossbills, arctic warblers, ruby-crowned kinglets, white-crowned and fox sparrows and dark-eyed juncos. Gray jays, chickadees, redpolls, ravens, three-toed woodpeckers and three owl species — boreal,

These travelers set up camp on the Sheenjek River several miles above Double Mountain. The river flows 200 miles from the heart of the Brooks Range to join the Porcupine River about 23 miles northeast of Fort Yukon. (William Wakeland)

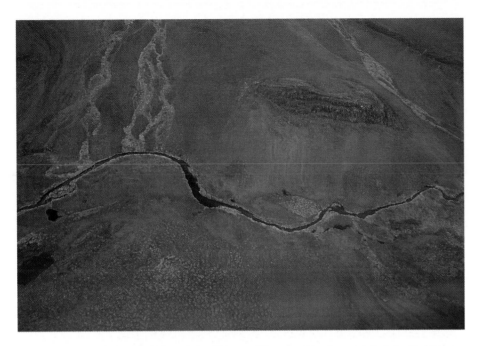

This aerial shows the Koness River headwaters east of Arctic Village in mid-August. The orange-red brush is dwarf birch; the yellow brush is willow. (David G. Roseneau)

great gray and northern hawk-owl — are year-round residents.

The Alaska section of the circumpolar boreal forest, sometimes referred to as the taiga after the Russian word for "land of little sticks," is a mixed band of conifers, primarily white and black spruce, with stands of paper birch and balsam poplar. The northern limit of the forest begins with a scattering of stunted spruce about 25 miles south of the headwaters of the major rivers. Timberline varies between 4,000 and 5,000 feet.

The Coleen and Firth rivers deviate from this pattern because their headwaters lie in much lower mountains. The upper Coleen supports the northernmost stands of white spruce for any southern drainage, while spruce border the north-flowing Firth to within a few miles of the arctic coast.

Traveling down the river valleys, the trees gradually grow more dense although broad open spaces speckle the forested landscape.

Poorly drained permafrost areas support scraggly black spruce, while well-drained rolling uplands are suitable for white spruce commonly reaching heights of 20 to 40 feet on southern slopes.

Spruce growing near the northern tree limit are the oldest trees in Alaska's Interior. They require many decades to grow because of the harsh climate and short growing season. Using an increment borer, Dennis and I once measured the age of several white spruce near our cabin. The trees ranged in diameter from three to seven inches, with their age determined largely by sun exposure. One three-inch white spruce growing in a shady location was 118 years old. Another spruce with the same diameter but growing on a sunny slope was 41. The oldest seven-inch spruce that we measured sprouted a few decades before the American Revolution.

Hiking beyond the spruce forest, we climb a few hundred feet toward the top of a nearby tundra-covered ridge. The ground is quilted with moss and lichen, dwarf birch and rhododendron, low-bush cranberry and bearberry, and Labrador tea, some blossoms of which I pick to brew later with black tea.

At the top of the ridge, Dennis and I find an explosion of blueberries at the 3,000-foot level. We pick a couple of pints, then soak in the last of summer's warmth. Temperatures are in the mid-60s, but within a few weeks the first snows will dust the forest and mountains. By October the average high temperature will drop to about 15 degrees, and by the end of November the sun will disappear for almost two months. While winter grips the land, frigid weeks of minus 50 degree weather are not uncommon. The average high doesn't rise above freezing until late April.

Leaving the ridge, we pause to gaze at the sweeping view before us. We stand near the edges of two ecosystems, in the transition zone known as the ecotone. To the north, a chain of peaks, valleys and undulating tundra-covered slopes begins. To the west, south and east, the boreal forest spreads across the floor of the Chandalar and Wind river valleys, each specked with innumerable lakes and ponds, with silvery threads of waterways meandering southwest to the distant Bering Sea. We scan for moose and caribou but see none on this day.

In the distance, a large patch of aufeis, or overflow ice, glistens along a nameless tributary of the Wind River. During the winter, aufeis forms as water runs over a frozen section of a river and freezes in successive layers. Underground springs often generate the overflow water. While some of this overflow ice melts and gradually disappears during the summer, other perennial ice sheets grow 10 to 15 feet thick and cover river channels for several miles. Aufeis can be found along numerous rivers on the north and south sides of the Brooks Range.

Heading back to the cabin, we spot three tundra swans flying overhead. Their white necks, gracefully outstretched, point south. As their white bodies disappear into the vast arc of blue, it reminds us that the white of winter will soon come of the Arctic Refuge.

Pilot Roger Dowding takes off on tundra tires from a gravel strip on the upper Sheenjek River. (Charlie Crangle)

Early Exploration

By Debbie S. Miller

The first people to explore what is now the Arctic Refuge were the ancestors of Inupiats and Athabaskans. These nomadic hunters lived in seasonal camps with good access to food resources. The Inupiat, who subsisted on both marine and land animals, lived in scattered settlements along the arctic coast. The inland Athabaskans, the Gwich'in (historically referred to as the Chandalar Kutchin), lived in seasonal camps on the south side of the Brooks Range. Camps were often located in places where migrating caribou could be intercepted, or along rivers and lakes where fish were plentiful.

While Native people have occupied the northeast corner of Alaska for more than 10,000 years, white explorers have arrived relatively recently. The first explorer to provide a written description of the region was Sir John Franklin (1786-1847) during his 1826 voyage in search of a northwest passage between Asia and Europe. In Franklin's *Narrative of a Second Expedition to the Polar Sea* (1828), he notes an unoccupied Inupiat settlement at Point Demarcation, which marks the eastern boundary of the Arctic Refuge, and separates Alaska from Canada:

"…This point seems to be much resorted to by the Esquimaux as we found many winter houses, and four large stages (sleds). On the latter were deposited several bundles of seal and deer skins, and several pair of snow-shoes. The snow-shoes were netted with cords

FACING PAGE: Tom Gordon opened a trading post on Barter Island in 1923 and used to bring his entire family by dog sled to this fishing hole, "Katak," on the Hulahula River. He had a house here for a while. This southernmost of three fishing holes on the Hulahula River is an important traditional and present-day fishing camp and base for sheep and caribou hunting. Gordon had opened a trading post at Demarcation Point in 1917, on behalf of whaler and trader Charles Brower for H.B. Liebes Co. of San Francisco. Gordon's brother-in-law Andrew Akootchook spent a winter trapping from Barter Island and helped Gordon open the trading post there. (Sverre Pedersen)

A member of Sir John Franklin's crew produced this illustration of Mount Copleston in the Shublik Mountains from their camp near the mouth of the Canning River in 1826. (Rare Book Collection #A1136, Alaska and Polar Regions Dept., University of Alaska Fairbanks)

of deer-skin, and were shaped like those used by the Indians near the Mackenzie...."

Franklin's description reflects the extensive trading network that existed between the Eskimos along Alaska and Canada's coast, and Athabaskans who traveled north from interior regions. Useful goods, such as iron pots, knives and beads, exchanged hands for many hundreds of miles; some items originated from Russian traders to the west at Kotzebue Sound. Others came from Hudson's Bay Co. traders to the east along the Mackenzie River corridor.

A few days later, Franklin's crew was forced to drag their boats across mud flats because sea ice hemmed them against the shore. On August 3, Franklin reached a frozen lagoon that he named Beaufort Bay (Beaufort Lagoon) after his friend Capt. Sir Francis Beaufort, hydrographer to the British Admiralty. At this point, Franklin discovered an open channel on the outside of the reef and the crew proceeded west. Soon they reached another trading site on a gravel reef near Point Griffin. Franklin wrote:

"...There were several huts on the reef, and one large tent, capable of holding forty persons, which appeared to have been lately occupied, besides eighteen sledges, that we supposed to have been left by the men who had gone from Herschel Island, to exchange their furs with the western Esquimaux. Among the baggage we found a spoon, made out of the musk ox horn, like those used by the Canadian voyagers...."

Closer to Barter Island, Franklin's crew had their first surprise encounter with Natives camped on the coast. Franklin had earlier employed an Eskimo interpreter, Augustus, who first spoke to the group of 54 people. Franklin describes the meeting:

"Beyond Point Manning, we descried a collection of tents planted on a low island, with many oomiacks, kaiyacks, and dogs around them. The Esquimaux being fast asleep, Augustus was desired to hail them, and after two or three loud calls, a female appeared in a stage of nudity; after a few seconds she called out to her husband, who awoke at the sound of her voice, and shouting out that strangers were close at hand, the whole space between the tents and the water was, in a few minutes, covered with armed, though naked, people...."

Franklin and his crew gave presents to these people who had traveled from Herschel Island, and he learned that they had just exchanged furs with western Eskimos, in return for iron and beads.

The explorer continued west along the arctic coast to the vicinity of Prudhoe Bay. Fearing that winter sea ice conditions might strand them, Franklin elected to retrace his route to the Mackenzie River on August 18. He named many of the land features of the Arctic Refuge along the way, such as the Romanzoff (now Romanzof) Mountains, honoring Count Nicholas Romanzoff, once chancellor of the Russian Empire. When the crew viewed the western terminus of the Sadlerochit and Shublik mountains (Franklin referred to them as the Rocky Mountains), Captain Back produced what is likely the first illustration of these mountains from their camp near the mouth of the Canning River.

After Franklin's voyage, a number of ships explored along the arctic coast, beginning with a Hudson's Bay Co.-sponsored expedition by P.W. Dease and Thomas Simpson in 1837. When Franklin mysteriously disappeared on his last expedition in 1845, ships searched for the *Erebus* and the *Terror* during a 10-year period. Perhaps Capt. Richard Collinson, commander of the H.M.S. *Enterprise* from 1850 to 1855, recorded the most extensive search.

Collinson notes in his journal that his crew spent a total of five years and 116 days looking for Franklin, leaving England in January 1850, crossing the oceans, then sailing northward along Alaska's and Canada's arctic coast, traveling as far as Victoria Strait in northern Canada before they turned back.

Collinson and crew spent three years in the Arctic without communication with the outside world. During summer 1854, Collinson spent time afoot in the Arctic Refuge, exploring the Canning River region and climbing the Sadlerochit Mountains. Collinson had hoped to climb to the summit of the Romanzof Mountains, but retreated when fog engulfed his climbing party in the Sadlerochits.

Somewhere near the mouth of the Canning, Collinson met 41 Inupiat. He reported the scene:

"They brought a good many fox and brown bear skins, but neither venison nor fish; these, however, they promised to return with, and produced three muskets, one of which had a date, 1850, on the lock; a few cartridges and some ball, both of which were highly prized, were given them, and a promise of more when they brought something in return...."

These Inupiat later returned with some Indians, then referred to as the Rat Indians. (They likely lived near the Rat River, a tributary of the Mackenzie River.) This Athabaskan group had carried messages from the crew of another boat, the H.M.S. *Plover*, from the arctic coast to the Hudson's Bay trading post at Fort Yukon, then returned north again to trade with the Inupiat.

Collinson described the Indians:

"These people were entirely different-featured from the Esquimaux, and were clad in blankets, and wore necklaces and ornaments through the septum of the nose. They were quiet, well-behaved people.... It is no doubt from them, and most likely from the Youcon [Yukon] establishment, that the Indians obtained firearms, as each of the men who visited us on this occasion was armed with a musket...."

While many vessels, like Collinson's, searched for the Franklin expedition along the arctic coast — a search not resolved until 1859 — the Hudson's Bay Co. was busy establishing its most western trading post at Fort Yukon. John Bell and Alexander Murray were the first white explorers to visit the middle Yukon region, traveling west from the Mackenzie River, and boating down the Porcupine

Ernest de Koven Leffingwell, at the wheel of the schooner Duchess of Bedford, *mapped Alaska's northeast coast and contributed important scientific information about the region's geology during his expedition of 1907 to 1914. With Leffingwell, left to right, are Ejnar Mikkelsen, Dr. Howe and Ejnar Ditlevsen. (Courtesy of Gill Mull)*

River to where it joined the Yukon. It was here, at the confluence of these two major watersheds, that this most distant fur-trading outpost was first established in 1847.

During the latter half of the 19th century, a steady trickle of trappers, traders, missionaries and gold miners explored and used resources of the southern portion of the Arctic Refuge. Yet, one of the greatest impacts on the wildlife resources was the hunting of caribou, Dall sheep and other game for the whaling fleet based at Herschel Island in the 1890s and early 1900s.

One of the best accounts of whaling along the arctic coast is recorded in Capt. John Cook's *Pursuing The Whale* (1926). Cook spent several winters anchored at Herschel Island and reported on the huge quantities of caribou and Dall sheep brought aboard for the whaling crews. In some cases, local Inupiat were hired to hunt for the crews. Other Natives bartered game and fish for desired trading goods. The Gwich'in living along the Porcupine River often brought sled loads of meat to the whalers via the Coleen and Firth river drainages.

This entry is one example of the many harvests noted on a daily or weekly basis:

November 15, 1903: "…three Itkilik (Indian) sleds came in from Rampart House with meat. One came to us with two hundred and thirty one pounds of deer meat, ten mink, and three marten skins. We paid them for same in tea, tobacco, powder, cartridges, lead, primers, matches, flour, and hard bread.…"

Oral history accounts from Arctic Village residents also include descriptions of many trading trips among the Gwich'in, Inupiat and whaling crews.

In 1905, Norwegian explorer Roald Amundsen followed the same trading route. After completing the first successful trip through the Northwest Passage from the Atlantic to the Pacific, Amundsen traveled from Herschel Island by dog team and skis up the Firth River, across the divide to the Coleen drainage and on to Fort Yukon along the Porcupine River trail. In 1919 Episcopal Archdeacon Hudson Stuck and explorer Vilhjalmur Stefansson also traveled this historic route.

Of the many early arctic explorers, perhaps geologist Ernest de Koven Leffingwell contributed the most scientific knowledge about the arctic coast in northeastern Alaska. From 1907 to 1914, Leffingwell accurately mapped the coast between Barrow and Demarcation Point, and studied the geology and topography of much of the refuge north of the Continental Divide. Leffingwell was based at Flaxman Island, having built a cabin

By erecting viewing towers, like this one at Demarcation Bay in the eastern Arctic Refuge near Canada, Eskimos and others who live and travel across the flat coastal plain gain an elevated vantage point to scan offshore for whales, ice openings or approaching weather. (Roger Siglin)

These grave markers recall a small Eskimo community that once occupied Brownlow Point, or Agliguagruk, on the northern tip of the Canning River delta. Fur trader Henry Chamberlain operated a trading post here from 1923 to 1943, one of the last on the Beaufort Sea. Brownlow Point was and continues to be an important summer and early fall fishing area, especially for arctic cisco. Otis Ahkivgak of Barrow in the late 1970s recalled moving here with his parents as a child in 1891 to fish. In the 1930s, Chamberlain disassembled geologist Ernest Leffingwell's home on Flaxman Island and moved it here to warehouse food, clothing and textiles. A visitor in 1933 described stone and turf houses inhabited by the Eskimos near the trading post. The 11 Eskimo graves here today include that of a 12-year-old boy who died in 1946 of an accidental gunshot wound. (George Wuerthner)

from the remains of the schooner *Duchess of Bedford*. This site is now on the National Register of Historic Places.

The first to describe permafrost features, Leffingwell mapped the Sadlerochit Formation, which later became famous as the reservoir for the Prudhoe Bay oil field. In Leffingwell's U.S. Geological Survey professional paper *The Canning River Region, Northern Alaska* (1919), it is clear that he had a holistic approach to his studies of the land. In addition to his scientific contributions in geography, geology and geomorphology, Leffingwell also described the natural history of what would become the refuge.

Alaska Division of Geological and Geophysical Surveys and former U.S. Geological Survey geologist Gil Mull points out that Leffingwell often worked alone, and on foot, in a remote area under extreme climatic conditions. "His unique survey was an incredible work of pioneering. No one has done that since," Mull reflected, with deep admiration for Leffingwell's contributions.

Indeed, while many other scientists would visit areas within the Arctic Refuge in future years, none would cover and study as much ground, nor produce such a detailed report as Leffingwell did. He will be remembered by scientists, and the Inupiat of that region, for years to come.

A Pioneer Visit
Mardy Murie and the Arctic Refuge
By Debbie S. Miller

Editor's note: *I first met Mardy Murie in Edmonds, Wash. in the mid-1970s, when she was in the Seattle area for the publication of a book of her husband, Olaus', bird sketches. In the early 1980s our paths crossed again, in Anchorage, when Mardy needed a ride to a friend's house and I had the available vehicle. Both times it was apparent that Mardy Murie is special, that she looks at the natural world and its wildness as do few others. This issue on the Arctic National Wildlife Refuge is a tribute, in part, to the observations, efforts and tenacity of Mardy Murie and her late husband.*

In summer 1926, Olaus and Mardy Murie, and their 10-month-old son, Martin, were exploring the northeastern corner of Alaska. Olaus Murie, a dedicated wildlife biologist, had been assigned by the U.S. Bureau of Biological Survey, predecessor of the U.S. Fish and Wildlife Service, to band geese along the Old Crow River.

Margaret E. (Mardy) Murie, still full of the wilderness spirit at age 90, reflected on their Old Crow trip from her log home in Moose, Wyo.

FACING PAGE: The wilderness of the upper Sheenjek near Lobo Lake, in the region of the Muries' 1956 expedition, today is part of the Arctic National Wildlife Refuge. The expedition made base camp part of the time on Lobo Lake, which they named for a gray wolf they observed along its shore. Mardy Murie wrote, in Two in the Far North, *that "...many people could see and live in and enjoy this wilderness in the course of a season, if they would just come a very few at a time... and then leave the camp site absolutely neat. It is possible, and this attitude of consideration, and reverence, is an integral part of an attitude toward life, toward the unspoiled, still evocative places on our planet. If man does not destroy himself through his idolatry of the machine, he may learn one day to step gently on his earth." (Charlie Crangle)*

"The Old Crow region was not an easy place. It took all of our stamina," she said, noting that many had dubbed it the "worst mosquito place in the world."

It took a full month of travel by boat to reach the small Athabaskan village of Old Crow at the confluence of the Old Crow and Porcupine rivers in Yukon Territory. The Muries and their friend Jess Rust left Fairbanks in late May, traveling down the silted Tanana River, then up the Yukon and Porcupine, across into Canada and on to Old Crow.

Their boat was the first to reach Rampart House on the Porcupine that summer, and when the Muries chugged into Old Crow, villagers ran to the river to catch their first glimpse of a white baby. In Mardy Murie's classic *Two in the Far North* (1978), she chronicles their Old Crow trip, and all the trials and fears of taking a baby into the wilderness. Most of the time Martin slept, played

Margaret E. (Mardy) Murie, 90, lives today at Moose, Wyo., in the middle of Grand Teton National Park.

She was born in Seattle to Minnie Fraser and cannery owner Ashton Thomas. They lived in Juneau for several years of her early childhood, until her parents divorced. Her mother remarried, to young lawyer Louis Gillette, and they returned to Seattle. When he became the new assistant U.S. Attorney for Fairbanks in 1911, 9-year-old Mardy and her mother joined him. She attended Fairbanks public schools, went to colleges Outside, then returned to Fairbanks to become the first woman graduate of the University of Alaska.

In Fairbanks the summer of 1921, after her second year at Reed College in Oregon, friends introduced her to Olaus Murie, a naturalist with the federal Biological Survey. Murie was in Alaska doing wildlife research.

In 1924, two months after graduating from UAF with a degree in business administration, Mardy, her mother and her best friend from college traveled down the Yukon River to meet Olaus. He was returning from summer bird research at the mouth of the Yukon. They married in a pre-dawn ceremony at the Episcopal log church in Anvik. The newlyweds spent their first 10 married days in Nulato, living in a tin-roofed cabin and traipsing around the nearby land, studying lemming and voles. Then they boarded a riverboat to journey up the Koyukuk River to Bettles, and on by dog sled to Wiseman and field camps in the Endicott Mountains of the Brooks Range to continue Olaus' caribou research.

This six-month winter adventure was the first of several extended trips they made together through the Alaska Bush. Mardy worked closely with Olaus during his years as a biologist with the U.S. Fish and Wildlife Service and, after 1946, as director of The Wilderness Society. After his death in 1963, she continued working for conservation causes and in 1976 was honored with a Doctor of Humane Letters degree from UAF. The Muries have two sons and a daughter, and Margaret enjoys visits by her 10 grandchildren and seven great-grandchildren. (Roger Kaye)

or drank from his bottle in a 4-foot wooden packing box, with the "rushing, relentless water right there beside us," Mardy wrote.

But there were some frightening times. On the Yukon River, the Muries put ashore at a fresh bear kill, and Mardy was left alone draping citronella-soaked cheesecloth over the baby as clouds of mosquitoes attacked them. She feared also that the bear might return to finish its moose calf meal. After heavy rains on the Old Crow, the Muries boated through some roaring rapids, with Martin squealing and reaching out at the white splash. When it was over and they were safe, Mardy wrote, "It seemed almost worth living with fear for a time, so sweet was its departure."

The Muries spent six weeks exploring the Old Crow drainage, sometimes surrounded by hordes of mosquitoes as they pulled and poled a scow and canoe for 250 miles to the river's headwaters after their motor broke the third day out from Old Crow. They often "sang their way" up the river, with Martin's diapers drying on a rack in the boat. In all this time they never saw another human being.

"It was a strange sensation being the only people in that country," Mardy reflected.

Yet the Muries were at home in this wilderness. Mardy wrote one day while alone on the river:

"...Nothing moved across the river on the green grass. Just the wilderness itself, friendly, and normal.... If I had spied a human form coming across the tundra, I would have been terrified; a bear or a wolf would have seemed excitingly normal...."

For a brief, breezy period when the Muries reached the headwaters there were no mosquitoes, and Martin was free to crawl around on the gravel bars, out of his harness.

"He walked on his hands and feet like a bear cub because the gravel hurt his knees," Mardy recalled, adding that when they later

Supreme Court Justice William O. Douglas, a prominent conservation leader of the time, joined the Murie expedition at Last Lake in the Sheenjek Valley. He is eating a fried grayling in this Aug. 2, 1956, photo. (George B. Schaller)

returned by steamer to Seattle, tourists were amused that Martin continued to walk on hands and feet.

Dr. Olaus Murie was the first wildlife biologist to explore the Old Crow and many other river drainages in northern Alaska, making several wildlife-study trips into the Brooks Range by dog team and boat. He carefully recorded his observations, and drew vivid illustrations that gained wide acclaim. Olaus and Mardy both thrived on their daily discoveries in the field, whether sighting a band of caribou, discovering a new flower or bird species, hearing a wolf or digging up a mammoth tusk or giant beaver tooth. All life forms and elements of the land were of constant interest.

Fred Dean, adjunct professor of wildlife management at the University of Alaska Fairbanks, reflected on Dr. Murie's scientific work.

"Olaus Murie was the first serious biologist who explored Alaska's Interior. He came here in the days when we knew very little, and he had a tremendous appreciation for wilderness. His extensive field studies on caribou, and other wildlife, and his

vivid illustrations were a major contribution," Dean said, noting that these early field studies became the foundation for Murie's conservation work.

The Muries had no idea, in 1926, that portions of the upper Porcupine and Old Crow rivers would one day be part of the Arctic National Wildlife Refuge. Nor did they know that in future years they would play a lead role in establishment of the refuge.

Thirty years later the Muries returned to northern Alaska after they had raised three children in Moose, Wyo., and studied extensively the elk of that area. In 1956, the New York Zoological Society and the Conservation Foundation sponsored an arctic expedition to the Sheenjek River valley under the leadership of Olaus Murie, then president of The Wilderness Society. The group spent two months exploring the flora, fauna and wilderness characteristics of the region. Their purpose was more than just science. Their scientific studies and accounts of their personal wilderness experiences would be the foundation for conservation efforts to establish an arctic preserve. [*See page 68 for more on the creation and political history of the Arctic Refuge.*]

By 1956 prominent conservationists such as Olaus Murie, Howard Zahniser, Sig Olson, Richard and Doris Leonard, Ira Gabrielson, Pink Gutermuth and many others had gotten behind the concept of an arctic preserve. This led to the Murie's 1956 expedition.

The Sheenjek party of scientists included Dr. Brina Kessel, a University of Alaska Fairbanks professor of zoology; and George Schaller and Robert Krear, two graduate students. Their scientific work resulted in numerous important publications on the region; their photos and films were later used to educate the public about this extraordinary wilderness and to successfully garner political support for an arctic preserve.

Again, Mardy Murie wrote vivid descriptions of the Sheenjek River valley and their daily discoveries in *Two in the Far North*. After climbing slopes covered with alpine tundra above Lobo Lake, she wrote:

"On top, across a carpet of mountain avens, heather, dwarf willows, and dozens of other lovely small plants, a balmy breeze blew. The sun was high and blazing. I lay flat on the moss and heather, hat over my face, and felt absolute content. Here I was, privileged to lie on top of a mountain in the Arctic, an observer of the richness of this short summer pageant.... The place, the scene, the breeze, the bird song, the fragrance of myriad brave burgeoning mosses and flowers — all blend into one clear entity, one jewel. It is the Arctic in its unbelievably accelerated summer life...."

After the 1956 trip, the Muries traveled widely, in and out of Alaska, giving slide shows and gathering grassroots support for the proposed preserve. Their personal campaign included a presentation

As a National Park Service planner in the early 1950s, George L. Collins nominated northeast Alaska for a wildlife sanctuary. His proposal, based on field surveys, quickly gained support of the Muries and other leaders in the conservation movement. In 1960, the area designated by Collins as worthy of protection was made the Arctic National Wildlife Range. Collins retired from the park service that year and helped found a consulting group called Conservation Associates. (Roger Kaye)

In 1956, Olaus and Mardy Murie made a two-month-long scientific expedition to the Sheenjek Valley, as part of the conservation effort to protect the northeastern corner of Alaska. Accompanying them were zoology professor Brina Kessel and graduate students Bob Krear and George Schaller. Left to right, Olaus, Bob Krear and Mardy eat dinner at a base camp on Last Lake. (George B. Schaller)

to Secretary of the Interior Fred Seaton, which strongly influenced Seaton's administrative action to establish the Arctic National Wildlife Range in 1960. On December 6 of that year, Seaton signed Public Land Order No. 2214, which established the 8.9-million-acre Arctic National Wildlife Range for its wilderness, wildlife and recreational values, by executive proclamation.

"We had a personal interest in the proposed arctic range, and we were determined to save it," Mardy reflected.

After the Muries received word that the Arctic Range had been established, Mardy wrote to Fairfield Osborn, director of the Conservation Foundation, describing their emotions: "We both wept — and I think then we began to realize what a long and complicated battle it had been."

In looking back at the many years of conservation work, Mardy refers to the Arctic Range victory as "the capstone," the crowning point of the Muries' endeavors to save America's wild places.

Bella Francis and Life on the Porcupine

By Roger Kaye

Editor's note: *Roger, of Fairbanks, is a pilot, free-lance writer and longtime friend of the Francis family.*

In her quiet, unhurried voice, Bella Francis recounted the travels of her teen years at Burnt Paw, the camp just a half-day's trip up the Porcupine River by dog team. Her words followed the steady rhythm of the needle she worked through the beaver mitt she sewed. Its unerring stitchwork was illuminated by the soft light of a kerosene lamp, the centerpiece of the rough-hewn table she leaned over. In the opposite corner of the aging cabin, her husband, Simon, just in from feeding the dogs, scraped fresh lynx pelts.

A few days earlier Bella and I had flown in to visit Simon and their son Charles at the camp they call Old Village: 105 miles up the Porcupine River from Fort Yukon, 30 miles from the nearest neighbor and a half century earlier, it seemed, than this late November evening of 1980.

I followed the winding route of her trap line on topographic maps as she described the lone journeys of her youth up the frozen Coleen River, across creeks, along sloughs and lakes, over hills. Many of her names for these features, I found, were not those the cartographer had used. Some were descriptive (creek with steep banks to climb), others were recalled by the hazards encountered (place where the ice is thin). She couldn't reckon distances in miles; travel was in terms of hours on the trail or nights from the home camp. But vivid memories — held 40 years then — had staked

FACING PAGE: *Bella Francis and son Charles hold lynx pelts at Old Village in 1980. Bella and husband, Simon, lived here during the first 11 winters of their marriage, from 1947 until 1958 when they moved to Fort Yukon to start the oldest of their three children in school. In 1967, they moved to Chalkyitsik on the Black River and visited Old Village during winter trapping trips until 1983. (Roger Kaye)*

John Herbert and May Martin Herbert, Bella's grandmother, were among the Indians living at Old Rampart in the 1920s. May, a Gwich'in from the Old Crow band, greatly influenced Bella's life. Bella's grandfather, Dick Martin, died before she was born. (Bella Francis photo; courtesy of Roger Kaye)

the trail in detail, and it was easy to measure the distance of her regular travel, about 90 miles.

Thirteen years later now, I still remember Bella's face that night as her dark eyes briefly turned from her work.

"Boy, I had fun those days! I always think back to it when I hear about women on those dog races."

Bella is a Gwich'in Athabaskan. She was born in 1928 at Old Rampart, a small trading post on the Porcupine River near the Canadian border. It had been abandoned by the Hudson's Bay Co.

in 1890 following a U.S. boundary survey determination that the British company was trespassing on American territory.

In the early '20s, a Swedish immigrant named Charlie Strom re-established the post. Soon it became the semipermanent base for eight or so wandering Indian families, including Bella's widowed grandmother May Martin and her children. When Bella was 1, Strom married her mother, Blanche, and became "the best father I could have."

Bella's grandmother was from the Old Crow band of Gwich'in. It was Grandma May, Bella recalls, who taught her domestic skills and most influenced her life. Born a nomad, May had lived through the end of the traditional era, but Bella recalls her talking more about the future than the past.

"When I was little I camp out with my grandmother lots. Sometimes she told me how they travel all around those old days, along the river or following the caribou. But not too many stories about old days, more about what we should do, what kind of people we should be."

Happy memories abound in Bella's recollections of her early childhood. "We were always busy those days — lots of things to do, even though we never have school." (Old Rampart was too small and isolated for a school.)

"Us kids were always outdoors, even if it's 50 below we're out playing. We liked to go sliding with a sled or little toboggan our dad made for us. Sometimes we slide down on our back. Caribou fur coat slides good, but it wears out. Boy, our moms get mad when they find out!

"Our moms made big caribou skin balls for us. They stuff it with hair. We played a game like football with it, sometimes by moonlight, late at night."

One of Bella's favorite winter pastimes was to play house with her girlfriends. They made their playhouse with blocks of wind-packed snow cut from the bank and stacked like an igloo. The girls pretended to be mothers; they fed their cloth dolls biscuits, donuts and caribou steaks from plates and bowls — all carved from snow. "We didn't have much toys those days," Bella said.

Most of the western goods found in the remote settlement came from her father's small store, which also served scattered families and lone trappers up and down the Porcupine and occasionally Eskimos from the arctic coast. Flour, rice, brown sugar, dried fruit, milk, eggs, rifles, ammunition and clothing materials were traded for hard-earned furs. Clothes were mostly homemade, recalls Bella. In winter, everyone dressed the same: caribou parkas, trimmed with wolf or wolverine, caribou pants and moose skin boots.

Bella is unhesitant when asked what possession was most valued. "Dogs. You gotta have good dogs those days. Gotta have good dogs for hunting, go trapping, haul your wood, haul your boat up the bank in fall time, everything. We take care of our dogs really good."

Mail came by dog team, every month or two. "Lots of excitement when the mail sled come up from Fort Yukon. We find out who died, who is married, who has baby." Bella's family was in on all the news, since people came over to have her father read them their letters.

The mail also brought her father's *Life* magazines, revealing that distant, magical, surreal world…the Lower 48.

"Us kids would just look at those pictures. We think it's summer all the time down there. We see all the interesting stuff they have. Lots of cars to drive around. Lots of movies. I wanted to go visit that place."

The Episcopal faith also arrived by dog team. Native ministers intermittently traveled downriver from Old Crow, Yukon Territory, or New Rampart on the border to hold services, baptize babies or marry people. Services were in Gwich'in and used translated bibles and hymnbooks. By her time, Bella said, most Indians were Christian, and pre-contact religious beliefs were no longer passed down.

Christmas was the highlight of the year, with the long-awaited celebration lasting past New Year's. Resident families who had dispersed to camps returned. Others from the Sheenjek and Black rivers arrived and, "for two weeks everybody forget all about trapping."

"We have big potlatch in community hall every evening, then everybody play games like stick pull. Sometimes they go a little crazy and grab people and threw 'em out in the snow."

In the early 1920s, Swedish immigrant Charlie Strom re-established the old Hudson's Bay Co. trading post of Old Rampart. He posed in front of a drying rack of salmon at Old Rampart for this picture by Bella's mother, Blanche, in 1937. Blanche married Charlie when Bella was 1. In 1965, Blanche was crippled by a stroke in Fort Yukon, where she lived until her death at age 67 in 1980. (Blanche Strom photo; courtesy of Roger Kaye)

Later, fiddlers played for square dances and the spirited Hudson's Bay reels, the Red River Jake being Bella's favorite. Between reels, a wind-up Victrola set the older folks waltzing and the younger fox-trotting. "Ah, we just dance and sing every night — sometimes way into the next morning.

"Us kids get lots of sweets that time — cookies, hard candy, all kinds of pies. They even make root beer for us. They make home brew for adults.

"We get lots of presents — new fur coat, slippers, mitts and snowshoes or toboggan when we get older."

Each June, Bella's family left the isolation of Old Rampart for two months in Fort Yukon, where her father waited for the steamboat *Yukon* to bring his trade goods for the next season. Before Strom brought his 40-foot plank boat around the last bend, he always put ashore so the family could change into their

TOP LEFT: *Bella Francis' mother, Blanche Strom, took this picture of Old Rampart in the mid-1930s. The first three large cabins from the front are: John and Mary Thomas' home; Charlie and Blanche Strom's home where Bella spent her childhood; and Strom's Trading Post. The community hall is the uppermost structure. The cabin at the right was occupied by Bella's grandmother, May Martin Herbert, after her second husband, John Herbert, died. The community also included a few cabins across the river, on the north bank. (Blanche Strom photo; courtesy of Roger Kaye)*

LEFT: *Bella and Simon's families posed with friends for this picture in 1933 at Old Rampart. From left to right: Bella's grandmother May Herbert; Alice John; Francis and Bella Adam, Simon Francis' parents; Bella's sister Doris Strom; Martha John (in doorway); Bella Strom (standing with hat and white blouse); David and Charlotte John (seated in front of doorway); Mary John holding her sister Florence; Jean Strom, Bella's sister; Charlie Strom, Bella's stepfather. (Bella Francis photo; courtesy of Roger Kaye)*

Simon Francis crosses a lake north of the Porcupine River, near his camp called Old Village, about 105 miles up the Porcupine River from Fort Yukon. Old Village appears on maps as John Herberts Village. This site is six miles west of the current refuge border, but much local subsistence activity occurs on the refuge. (Roger Kaye)

best clothes. "It was like going to a big city to us." Bella said.

"When we come to the bank (at Fort Yukon), people start hollering and everybody comes to see us and shake hands.

"The first thing us kids do is eat some fresh stuff our auntie saved for us. Oranges, apples — boy they're good that time."

In August, they loaded the boat for the long trip upriver. "We had fun visiting, but we need to get back home and do our things to get ready for winter."

Each fall Bella was able to help more. By the time she was 12, she had three sisters and a brother to watch. She recalls coaxing and carrying them up the steep hill behind the settlement to pick blueberries, cranberries, crowberries and raspberries. Their harvest, about 35 gallons, was stored in wooden kegs in the cellar underneath the cabin. "We eat berries all winter, so we pick lots."

After the fall runs of chum and king salmon began, Bella's job was to help cut and dry the 1,000 fish netted for food and more importantly, to fuel their ravenous dog team through the winter.

In September, when her father returned from hunting with his boat loaded with moose or caribou, Bella helped her mother and grandmother cut, dry and smoke the meat. She learned to prepare sinew for thread and string, and to repair snowshoes. The women pounded dried meat with a round rock, mixed it with marrow and berries and boiled the mix to make pemmican for the trail. "It's real tasty," Bella said, "I still make it today."

Change came to the lifeway of the upper Porcupine quickly in the late 1930s. For Bella, the most memorable event occurred in 1937 when the first airplane landed at Old Rampart. Her mother, pregnant with her last child, decided to have the baby at the hospital in Fort Yukon. Earlier, Bella's father had sent word to have

pioneer bush pilot Jim Dodson come up to fly his wife to town. They decided that Bella and her sister would accompany their mother.

An expectant crowd came running as Dodson's ski plane skidded to a stop on the river ice. "Everyone is interested, but they are scared for us to go in it. ...I told my Mom, 'I don't like it, let's go with the dogs instead.'"

The takeoff remains embedded in Bella's memory. "Oh, it was scary. My sister Doris is screaming. We all just hang on to each other and hope it don't crash."

An hour later they landed safely. But to this day Bella has an abiding distrust of small airplanes. When she flies, she carries a small

Bella Francis' family home was the only building remaining at Old Rampart, on the Porcupine River, in 1981. The Porcupine was the original gateway to the middle Yukon River region. Scottish trader John Bell traversed the Yukon Territory and followed the Porcupine down to its confluence with the Yukon River in 1844, becoming the first white man to report sighting the middle Yukon. (Judy Liedburg, USFWS)

can with rabbit snares, fishhooks, a knife, soup cubes, cocoa and aspirin. "If the motor quit and I'm alive, I'll have something to eat anyway."

Boats with motors were coming upriver more often by then, increasing contact with Fort Yukon. Each year the town's school, hospital, stores and easier life drew more families from the river. By 1941 only three families remained at Old Rampart and Strom's trading post closed.

The Strom family didn't want to leave the Porcupine though.

They decided to move downriver 35 miles where the trapping was better, and settled into a relative's camp called Burnt Paw.

"Those were my best days…." Bella's words trailed off, resonating silently in my mind, and, I'm sure, in Simon's too. She lay down her beaver mitt and turned.

"After we move to Burnt Paw, then I have my own trap line. I have my own dogs, nine good dogs.

"I was teenager then, first time without my dad. Everything I catch is for the family. When I was 16, I catch almost $3,000. I was proud.

"Sometimes Simon used to bring the mail up to us and visit but I didn't pay any attention to him. I'm too busy."

Simon responded that he used to stop by because Burnt Paw was near the end of his trap line. He added that he didn't pay much attention to her, either.

Bella continued. "I really enjoy myself out alone with my dogs. When you go alone you can go long ways. Get up early, nobody to wait for, rest when you want, make camp when you want."

Those days of independence and adventure, however, were not to last. In June 1947, while in Fort Yukon, Bella's father told her he wanted to have a talk. He was 66, and his asthma was worsening; he wouldn't be able to go back up to Burnt Paw.

"Bella," he told me, "You're 19. It's time for you to get married. He know I don't like it. I wanted to go back to my trap line. And I was shy toward men. But those days we do what our parents want. He said, 'I want you to marry him.'" Bella shot a laughing glance toward the man who had brought the mail to Burnt Paw.

Simon only smiled, continuing to comb the lynx skin he had just pulled onto a stretcher.

Simon and Bella were married on the Fourth of July. They decided to live at Simon's camp, Old Village. It was their home from August through May for the next 11 years. Daughter Josie was born in 1950, Linda came in '52 and Charles in '54.

They continued the seasonal cycle they had been born to. Simon hunted moose and caribou in the fall and set nets for salmon. Bella prepared the fish and meat, skinned, tanned and sewed while taking care of the kids. In winter, when Simon left for week-long runs of the trap line, Bella's travels were confined to short rabbit and muskrat lines near the cabin, pulling a toboggan with small, impatient children.

"I liked my kids, but that was the hardest thing, when I can't go out on the trap line."

In 1957, when Josie turned 7, Simon and Bella made a hard decision: they would move to Fort Yukon so their children could attend school.

Vividly, Bella recalls the spring trip downriver that would be their last. Their 30-foot plank boat, powered by a sturdy nine horsepower Johnson motor, was loaded to the gunwales with three children, seven dogs, dried fish, the winter's fur catch and provisions for a week. Along the way they camped at old muskrat-hunting areas.

"As soon as the boat is tied up, Simon leaves for hunting. The dogs are howling, kids are crying and I have to set up camp. Some nights Simon gets 50 or 100 rats (muskrats) and I stay up all night skinning. Lots of work, but oh, I miss it."

An era ended with that trip in 1957. The Francis family was the last to leave the trapping-based seasonal cycle that had dominated the Porcupine for nearly 80 years.

Simon and Bella found life in Fort Yukon stressful, and bad for their kids because of increasing alcoholism in the town. In 1962 the Francises and four other families returned to the Porcupine to establish a new, dry village 27 miles above Burnt Paw. Canyon Village began with 10 adults and enough kids for a school.

The dream of returning to the old ways was short-lived, however. By 1967, five years later, the number of students fell below the 13 required by the Bureau of Indian Affairs for a school, and Canyon Village was abandoned. The Francises moved to Chalkyitsik, a small village on the Black River 30 miles south of the Porcupine. For 16 trapping seasons, Simon, Charles and later Simon Jr. traveled back and forth from Chalkyitsik to Old Village. Bella visited occasionally, but the river was never home again.

Today, she and Simon stay in Fairbanks to be near the hospital. They are often invited to talk to school classes and youth groups about their early experiences. Recently they served as Native Elders-in-Residence at the University of Alaska, teaching about Athabaskan cultural traditions.

Visits to their small apartment usually find Bella busy making fancy beaded slippers or functional gloves, mukluks, mitts or fur hats for sale. She still talks as she sews, but now, I listen as her youthful soul speaks through a tired body. "Even now," she recently told me, "I still want to go back to Porcupine River. If I'm healthy, I'll move right back."

Bella, shown here in 1991 checking salmon in her smokehouse at Fort Yukon, was raised in the Porcupine River valley and grew up using the subsistence resources of what is now the southern portion of the Arctic Refuge. (Roger Kaye)

At Home in the Wilderness

By Roger Kaye

Editor's note: *For years the Richard Hayden family maintained two main camps, a summer one and a winter one, in their subsistence lifestyle on the south slope of the Brooks Range. But the Haydens decided to spend summer 1993 in Fairbanks. Roger, of Fairbanks, is a long-time friend of the Hayden family.*

Deep in the isolation of the Arctic National Wildlife Refuge, in a cabin hidden among tall spruce edging the Sheenjek River, the Hayden family takes an unaccustomed break from their routine. Today, they have visitors. This is an unusual occasion—particularly in December—for a family that may be among the most isolated in the United States, whose nearest neighbor is three days away by dog team, and who often sees months pass between visiting planes.

My wife, two daughters and I had flown in to spend the weekend with the Haydens, to do some cross-country skiing, and mostly to enjoy their hospitality and different-drummer lifestyle.

Life here is tough. Winters are among the most extreme in the state along these southern foothills of the Brooks Range, more than 100 miles north of the Arctic Circle. Amenities are few, and the subsistence lifestyle takes on a meaning with consequences seldom found anymore in Bush Alaska.

Caribou, moose and fish are Haydens' staples. Trapping provides a meager cash income—their bridge linking a lifestyle of yesteryear with the necessities of today. Still, that limited income and costly air charters combine to keep them chronically short of store-ordered supplies. Hunger, hardship and uncertainty have tested them often during the last 21 years.

FACING PAGE: *Duane Hayden gets a ride as the older Hayden siblings haul two kegs of water home over the frozen river. They made the caribou skin parkas, boots and mitts that they are wearing. (Roger Kaye)*

ABOVE: *The Hayden family at their summer camp are, left to right, Susan, Richard Sr. holding Duane, Richard Jr., Shannon holding Judy Ann, and Daniel. (Stuart Pechek)*

RIGHT: *Richard Hayden Sr. builds a dog sled. (Roger Kaye)*

Even in Alaska, families with this level of dependence on the land are rare these days. But that's not what is most unusual about the Haydens. Most intriguing is the fact that these ardent hunters and trappers are, at the same time, committed environmentalists and wilderness supporters.

"We consider ourselves environmentalists," Richard Hayden Sr. says, "even though we can't be active in any of those organizations. I know a lot of those who live out like us don't agree, but I've come to see that people need to be more careful of the land and more mindful of the future."

He mentions the many letters he has written to representatives and agencies throughout the years, urging more protective provisions for the region. "We'd like to see our area designated as wilderness, with regulations that will keep it that way."

I ask if regulation isn't at variance with the freedom and independence that seem to characterize the hunting/trapping lifestyle. He thinks about that for a minute. "Well, to live free, that's why I came out here. But it's more important to us to be free in country left natural than it is to be free to do anything we want. You can't have both these days."

He offered an example. "It used to be that we could cut timber wherever we wanted. Now, cutting trees along the river like we used to isn't allowed. That makes it a little harder for us, but it protects the shoreline. With more people on the river, it just wouldn't look the same a hundred years from now without that regulation."

To some, Hayden's sensitivity toward the land and sense of restraint is tree-hugger extremism; to others it's just good stewardship. U.S. Fish and Wildlife Service biologist Fran Mauer has been studying the caribou, moose and sheep populations of the Arctic Refuge for 12 years. He often stops by Haydens' camp in the course of his surveys. "Richard is unusual in that he's been able to look way beyond his immediate self-interest to the bigger picture, what's sustainable in the long term. He weighs what he does and what he supports against a conviction that this area should always remain wild."

That evening, after the dogs were fed, we all sat down to enjoy a caribou roast. Richard and his wife, Shannon, ask us about the goings on in Fairbanks. Richard Jr., 18, Daniel, 16, and Susan, 15, tell us about their recent adventures. Duane, 4, and Judy Ann, 1 and 1/2, are anxious to get into the ice cream they caught us unloading. The temperature is dropping precipitously outside, but the homemade barrel stove keeps the small cabin comfortably warm. Above it, lines strung between spruce log beams hold drying socks, gloves, caribou mukluks and mitts. From nails in the log walls hang parkas, sweaters, rifles, dog harnesses and a variety of tools. Shelves made of rough-cut spruce planks hold pots and pans, ammunition, sewing materials, candles and odds and ends. On the bookshelf, trapping catalogues and hunting books oddly coexist with a few titles like *The Rights of Nature.*

Judged by conventional standards, the winter home of the six Haydens is crowded, cluttered and spartan, probably indigent if a social worker were to come and rate it. But within is a richness, a gregarious family intimacy and an uncommon sense of cooperation born of the real need for each member's contribution.

Richard Sr. shuts down the harsh light of the family's Coleman lantern and touches a match to the wick of a kerosene lamp. White gas, he says, is too expensive to burn when kerosene will do. He is a smallish man with hard muscles and sharp features that go suddenly soft when the white light from the Coleman is replaced by a warm lamp-glow. As if it were a campfire, we focus on the lamp's flame, flickering across our faces in the dark cabin. Richard talks of his past.

"I was still a teenager when I figured out that I was ill-suited to mainstream life," Richard says. At 18 he lit out from his Minnesota home to become a trapper like those he had read about in outdoor magazines. He tried Canada, then settled on the Little Susitna in southcentral Alaska, later moving to the Nabesna River. But at each place, he says, he was pushed out by roads, snow machines and commercialization. Like Daniel Boone, he kept moving. In 1969 while hitchhiking through Whitehorse, Yukon Territory, he met Shannon, a Tlingit Indian. After a year-long correspondence

Little Duane Hayden brings in firewood for his mom, Shannon.
(Roger Kaye)

courtship, they were married and moved to their present home.

As we talk, Shannon strings colorful beads onto short lengths of monofilament fish line, meticulously creating a rainbow spectrum. She is finishing a bead-and-caribou-skin sun catcher, one of the seven we will take back to town to sell for her. Her manner shows the quiet, unassuming grace of a traditional Native woman. The miles that separate her family from civilization are not threatening, she says, but barriers from undesirable influences. And the shared work—hauling water, feeding dogs, making and repairing clothing and the ever-present need to cut, haul and split firewood—helps keep the family close.

Years ago, Shannon gave up helping her husband with the hunting and trapping to devote full-time to her multiple occupations of homemaker, mother and teacher. The children have never gone to school. The older three are enrolled in a correspondence course. Three or four times a year a teacher flies in to provide guidance. Their mother assists, but does not take charge; how and when the lessons are completed are the children's responsibility.

"I know there are a lot of things our kids miss out on," Shannon

admits. "Like school and social activities. But they aren't exposed to drugs and drinking and all that either. Out here, they have a healthy start in life."

The oldest three now provide nearly half the family's fur income, with Susan being the most enthusiastic trapper. Born in a linecamp upriver, she has accumulated an impressive repertoire of bush skills. When coaxed, the pretty, black-haired teen modestly acknowledges that somewhere between 30 and 35 caribou have fallen to her .270 Remington. Her proudest moment, she says, was when she caught her first wolverine—at age 12.

While this talkative teen can carry on about guns, hunting and trap sets with the authority of a seasoned woodsman, her main interest—her true love—is her dog team. Five barrel-chested, 85- to 95-pound working huskys.

"Mushing is what I like more than anything. That's why I like winter best, because we go on long trips and camp out."

Sometimes Susan and one of her brothers run the 70-mile trap line, overnighting in tent camps. Each trip poses hazards and hardships: thin river ice, overflow, broken toboggans, fighting dogs and the ever-present possibility of the temperature dropping past 50 below. Darkness accompanies them most of the time.

They return with marten to skin, and sometimes a fox, lynx or wolverine. But never wolves.

"We used to trap wolves," explains Richard. "But the more I would see them and follow them, the more I saw them as different from other fur. They're the spirit of this country, the wildness of it. One came into the dog yard and killed a pup last year, so I had to shoot it. Otherwise, we leave them alone. The kids feel the same way, especially since some of the dogs are half wolf."

Around the last week in March, the family leaves this five-month home on the river for the main camp on a large lake 40 miles to the west—a two-day journey by dog team. Main camp is similar to winter camp but closer to tree line and surrounded by smaller

Daniel Hayden removes a whitefish from the net while Richard Jr. watches. This day's catch will feed the family's dogs. (Roger Kaye)

Richard Hayden Sr. hands Susan some moose meat from the cache. (Roger Kaye)

and thinner spruce stands. Moving between camps allows the Haydens to harvest from different animal populations, thereby avoiding local over-harvest.

By mid-April, wet and melting snow prevents dog team travel, restricting the Haydens' range as well as the resources they can exploit. They hunt ptarmigan and grouse on foot and catch fish through the ice. Before the lake ice breaks up, a bush pilot delivers one or two ski-plane loads of dog food and all other supplies that will be needed before freezeup in late October.

Summer is a time to work around the cabin. Mosquitoes and gnats, bogs and tussocks conspire to make extended travel too formidable. Fish nets are repaired and set in the lake. Whitefish and pike are fed to the dogs and eaten by the family both fresh and dried. Coltsfoot plants are gathered and eaten. Caribou skins harvested the previous fall are tanned and made into mukluks, mitts, sleeping pads and parkas. Each family member makes his or her own winter clothing. The country is hard on clothes, but the five older Haydens are skilled skin sewers. Parkas require about 10 hours of skin preparation and eight hours of sewing.

Shannon knits sweaters, socks and mukluk liners, some of which are sent out by plane to be sold in town. The kids try to catch up on school work neglected during the winter and spend hours each day repairing toboggans, dog harnesses, tow lines and other gear.

In early fall, caribou returning from their calving grounds on the North Slope can usually be found migrating along the ridge tops above main camp. Caribou are the family's mainstay, the single most important food and primary material for winter clothing. After sighting the first groups, the family moves uphill to caribou camp, a wall tent pitched on a ridge top. In a typical year, two-thirds of the 25 to 30 caribou they require are taken on this hunt. These will be the skins prepared for tanning, as the skins of the winter caribou are too long-haired and heavy for practical use. Dried meat, for use throughout the year, is made from the first

dozen or so animals. During slack periods in hunting, 10 gallons to 20 gallons of blueberries, lowbush cranberries and cloudberries are picked.

In late October, as soon as the creeks freeze and enough snow accumulates for mushing, the Haydens return to the Sheenjek. While waiting for the November 1 opening of the trapping season, they speculate on fur prices, ironically determined by the whims of wealthy women a world away whose desire for luxury apparel

Daniel and Richard Sr. untangle dog harnesses at the Hayden family's main winter trapping camp in the southern foothills of the Brooks Range. (Roger Kaye)

provides the economic basis for this contrasting lifestyle.

"We're always on the edge of being broke," Richard says as our conversation drifts to the privations of living against the tide of civilization. "We teach the kids to make as much of what they use as possible to minimize the use of money."

"And everything is used economically," adds Shannon. Her comment reminds me of the well-crinkled aluminum foil on the shelf behind her. It could probably hold a record for use and reuse.

By necessity they improvise. When lamp fuel ran out one winter, light came from Eskimo-style grease lamps made of melted tallow and cotton wicks. Earlier this winter Daniel wore out his last pair of gloves. After making a pattern, he sewed a pair from the material of an old pair of pants.

"We've only felt hard times a few times," says Richard. "Those were years when hardly any caribou came through. When the meat runs low it's hard to work in the cold. We just stretch out."

"Stretching out" is Hayden parlance for rationing and going

hungry. I remembered an example several years ago during an early spring visit. As usual, as soon as my plane stopped on the ice the kids were there. But customary greetings were foregone and replaced with, "What did you bring to eat?" They had been getting by with a meager daily allotment of dried meat and bread. It had been hard to see hungry kids, but that hardship also passed.

As the hour grows late, our conversation returns to the Haydens' thoughts on use and protection of the wilderness and their vision of the value it holds for the rest of the nation.

When Richard Sr. first came into the country, its remoteness was its protection. That time is past, he fears. "The future is threatening. The oil companies want to develop on the other side of the range. We see more people come to hunt, float and hike, and some aren't very careful with the country. If they ever put a road through here, it would never be the same."

"I don't think we are so poor a nation that we can't set this area aside from exploitation and overuse," Richard concludes. "If we don't, we're just stealing from our children and their children."

The Haydens are a vestige of a bygone era, a living American cultural resource. Perhaps they, like the wolves that run unharmed over their trap line, are symbols of this last great wilderness, the Arctic Refuge.

LEFT: *Susan Hayden plays with one of her wolf-hybrid sled dogs. Mushing her five-dog team is her favorite activity. (Roger Kaye)*

BELOW: *Richard Hayden Sr. and Susan set up a tent camp along the trap line. A tent and sleeping bags are always carried in the sled. (Roger Kaye)*

Kaktovik

The only town within the Arctic National Wildlife Refuge is Kaktovik (*KakTOEvik*), on Barter Island at the refuge's northern edge.

Most of Kaktovik's 225 residents are Inupiat Eskimos. They have experienced many changes in recent years, mostly associated with oil development on the North Slope. Oil has brought jobs, a new high school with a gym and swimming pool, a power plant, street lights, new homes. It has also brought

Kaktovik is the only permanent settlement within the Arctic National Wildlife Refuge. This north-northeasterly view shows the ice of the Beaufort Sea in the distance, beyond Bernard Spit. (David G. Roseneau)

outsiders competing for lands and waters that have sustained the Inupiat for centuries.

The people of Kaktovik keep busy all year with traditional activities. They often spend weekends and vacations at family hunting and fishing camps along the coast and in the northern part of the Arctic Refuge.

They hunt ducks and geese in late spring, bearded and hair seals in summer. They fish for arctic whitefish and char in coastal lagoons, and in winter travel by snow machines to traditional fishing camps along the Hulahula River. They hunt caribou along the coast in summer, and in the foothills and mountain valleys in winter. Also in winter, they go into the mountains to hunt Dall sheep and trap fox, wolves and wolverines.

But of everything, whaling is perhaps Kaktovik's most important community activity. Each fall, Inupiats from Kaktovik hunt bowhead whales during their westerly migration. Practically everything in town shuts down. Most men and some women go out in boats, sometimes as far as 20 miles offshore. Everyone helps with butchering, and they share the meat and fat according to tradition.

Barter Island has long served as a trade center for Eskimos of Alaska and Canada and Indians from the south.

In early times, the island was inhabited by whale hunters; numerous whale bones surrounded prehistoric sod house sites where the airport is now located. These people were driven off by Inupiat from the west, according to legend. During this fight, a couple's only son was killed and they fished his dead body from the water with a

seining net; Kaktovik means "seining place."

Later, the island was used for seasonal camps by Eskimos who hunted and fished along the coast. By the late 1800s, commercial whalers were stopping here regularly. In 1923, a trading post opened to buy fox furs.

Around this time, the government brought about 2,000 reindeer to the coastal plain south of Barter Island. Local families managed the herds and were paid in reindeer. Harsh winters in the mid-1930s brought near starvation. Efforts to rebuild the herd failed in 1938, when 3,000 reindeer driven from Barrow turned around just as they reached the Camden Bay area. They stampeded home, taking most of the remaining Barter Island herd with them.

LEFT: *This Kaktovik resident slices a piece of muktuk, skin and blubber cut earlier from a bowhead whale. (Sverre Pedersen)*

BELOW: *An Inupiat Eskimo boy at Kaktovik finishes off an ice cream cone. The Inupiat of Kaktovik mix contemporary and traditional lifestyles. Many modern conveniences have come to the village since development of North Slope oil fields, yet Eskimo families continue a centuries-old subsistence culture that includes whaling in the Beaufort Sea and hunting and fishing within the Arctic National Wildlife Refuge. (Chlaus Lotscher)*

The Inupiat of Kaktovik consider whaling their most important community and cultural activity, but they also hunt caribou. These women butcher caribou in Kaktovik. (Sverre Pedersen)

In 1945, the government started mapping the coast and hired a few local people. After World War II, Barter Island became a radar site for the Distant Early Warning (DEW line) system. Kaktovik families had to relocate their village three times between 1947 and 1964, during the military build-up. Jobs on the DEW line and the opening of a school made Kaktovik the area's central settlement by

the 1950s; before that people lived scattered throughout the region in several dozen coastal and river sites.

In 1969, residents helped reintroduce musk ox to the coastal plain. The animals arrived on cargo planes in wooden crates. Villagers hauled one group across the island on sleds attached to snow machines. Some of the animals wandered out onto the sea ice, but villagers drove them back. The original transplanted herd has grown to more than 550 animals: 350 musk ox live in the northern refuge with the overflow dispersed outside refuge boundaries, east into Canada and west toward Prudhoe Bay.

The oil strike at Prudhoe Bay brought a new type of attention to the area. Each year, oil exploration moves closer to Kaktovik, with drilling offshore near Barter Island and proposals to open the Arctic Refuge coastal plain.

The Kaktovik Inupiat Corp. and the Arctic Slope Regional Corp., for-profit Native corporations created by the 1971 Alaska Native Claims Settlement Act, own land in the refuge and support oil leasing on the coastal plain. The North Slope Borough, the regional government, collects taxes from the oil fields that have helped pay for improvements in Kaktovik. The borough supports drilling.

Not everyone in Kaktovik agrees with the official Inupiat position. "There are 200-and-some people and 200-and-some different opinions," said Kaktovik mayor Marx Sims, taking a quick break from unpacking ice cream at his store one afternoon.

The Inupiats do agree on one thing: They do not want offshore oil development, because of possible disruptions to whale migrations and other threats to culturally important marine mammals.

In recent oil leasing debates, Kaktovik saw plenty of action. It became a popular stopover for oil company executives, reporters, and Congressional tour groups en route to the Arctic Refuge. Public meetings between villagers and visitors occurred often.

Today, outfitters and government biologists are among those who operate out of Kaktovik. Some local residents say they want to start guiding trips into the refuge, their traditional homelands.

Arctic Village, a community of about 125 Gwich'in Athabaskan Indians, sits on the East Fork Chandalar River, just outside the Arctic National Wildlife Refuge on the south slope of the Brooks Range.

It is one of about 15 Gwich'in villages across northeast Alaska and northwest Canada, and the closest Indian village to the refuge. The people of Arctic Village hunt and fish on the refuge and adjacent tribal lands. Their nearest neighbors are the Gwich'in of Venetie on the Chandalar River, about 100 miles south by plane or snow machine.

The first cabin in Arctic Village, or *Vashraii K'oo* in Gwich'in, was built in 1908 by Chief Christian. Ten years later on a bluff above the river, an Episcopal log church was built, supervised by Albert Tritt, the Gwich'in's first Episcopal lay reader.

For the most part, the Gwich'in were seminomadic until the 1950s. They hunted and traveled between seasonal settlements and camps located along the Sheenjek River

The mountains of the Arctic National Wildlife Refuge are visible from Arctic Village, a community of mostly Gwich'in Athabaskan Indians on the East Fork Chandalar River at the refuge's southern border. Although hundreds of miles from Alaska's highway system, Arctic Village has a local road. (George Matz)

and places such as Old John Lake, Christian, Venetie and Arctic Village, where a cluster of log cabins had gone up around the church. The first school in Arctic Village opened in 1947, and more Gwich'in families began staying year-round. The growth continued through the 1950s, and in 1959 the Bureau of Indian Affairs built a new school.

Today, Arctic Village remains a small community on the river's east bank, with

homes, a post office, health clinic, school and store. The log church is on the National Register of Historic Places.

The Gwich'in historically traded with Inupiat Eskimos on the arctic coast, traveling along the rivers by foot or dog sled 300 miles round-trip. They took things such as wolverine skins and spruce pitch to trade. After the mid-1800s, when white whalers reached the arctic coast, the Gwich'in traded

for rifles, ammunition, tobacco and other manufactured items.

But more than anything else, Gwich'in survival depended on caribou for food, clothing and culture. As the continent's northernmost Indians, the Gwich'in trace thousands of years of ancestry to the region and its Porcupine caribou herd. They call themselves "people of the caribou."

The Porcupine herd's annual migration covers a region of more than 96,000 square miles, from the boreal forests of the Chandalar, Porcupine and Peel river drainages across the Brooks Range to the arctic coastal plain. Most calving takes place within a two- to three-week period east of the Hulahula River, in snow-free areas of tussock uplands. The vegetation apparently camouflages the calves from a relatively few number of wolves and other predators, and calf survival is better. The coastal plain also provides nutritious forage for adult caribou, replenishing their energy reserves after the stresses of winter, pregnancy, migration, birth, lactation, hair molt, antler growth and insect harrassment. As swarms of mosquitoes emerge, the caribou gather in dense groups and move into the wind at the northern edge of the coastal plain.

Beginning in mid-August each year as the animals return south, the western branch of the herd passes close to Arctic Village. The

ABOVE LEFT: *These Gwich'in women prepare caribou for a feast in Arctic Village. This meat, served in a variety of ways, is a staple food of the Gwich'in. (George Matz)*

ABOVE: *Martha James, a Gwich'in elder in Arctic Village, enjoys some roasted caribou ribs during a 1991 gathering of indigenous people from all over the world for the International Indian Treaty Council. The meeting was held in Arctic Village to focus attention on the Gwich'in's concern over the future of caribou and their habitat in the Arctic National Wildlife Refuge. (Karen Jettmar)*

first caribou are allowed to pass undisturbed, and then hunting begins. Villagers hunt from camps near timberline and along the rivers by boat.

Before rifles, the Gwich'in used arrows and spears or drove the animals off steep cliffs. Their main method of hunting large numbers of caribou was erecting wooden fences in strategic locations to channel the animals into corrals. The use of fences ended around the turn of the century. Remains of these fences, some estimated more than 300 years old, appear oriented to intercept modern caribou movements, indicating that the herd's migration has changed little.

The animals traditionally provided meat for food, bone for tools, sinew for thread and rope, hides for clothing, bedding and shelter. Today, although most clothes and tools are bought, caribou hides are made into winter boots, leggings, blankets and traditional crafts. Caribou bone scrapers are still made and used in preparing the hides. The meat is a staple, preserved by freezing and drying. Roasted caribou heads are considered a delicacy. Some elders save caribou hooves, remembering past times of near-starvation when broth made by boiling hooves provided the only nourishment. Caribou remain central to Gwich'in culture and are the subjects of songs, stories and dance.

Because of their reliance on the caribou, the Gwich'in oppose oil leasing on the coastal plain.

They first argued against it in the late 1970s, when a small group of Gwich'in went to Washington, D.C. They began working for international habitat protection, helping negotiate the United States-Canada Porcupine caribou herd agreement and the creation of its advisory International Porcupine Caribou Board.

In 1988, as the oil leasing debate again erupted, the Gwich'in nation met at Arctic Village, the first such conclave in a century. From this came the Gwich'in Steering Committee, directed "to establish Gwich'in cultural survival as a major issue in the debate over oil development" in the Arctic Refuge.

The eight-member committee, working from a cramped two-room headquarters in Anchorage on a small budget, has taken the Gwich'in message to lawmakers and the public.

"We depend on the caribou for our food, clothing, tools, our stories, our dance," said Sarah James, a leader from Arctic Village. "If development disturbs the herd in their calving area, decreases their number, or changes their migration, it affects us. We want to protect them."

Margaret Tritt works on her caribou hides in Arctic Village. (Dennis Miller)

A Future in Question

Nowhere in Alaska has the tug-of-war between resource development and preservation of wilderness been fought as intensely as on the coastal plain of the Arctic National Wildlife Refuge. For years, the oil industry and conservation organizations have battled over opening the coastal plain to oil leasing.

At stake for the oil industry is the nation's most promising onshore petroleum prospect. Oil seeps, oil-stained sandstone outcroppings and oil-bearing shales throughout the coastal plain hint at potentially large reservoirs underneath. No one knows how large, but estimates peg recoverable reserves at 600 million to 9 billion barrels with the mean at 3.2 billion barrels, the third largest find in U.S. history.

"The next battle…will be the fight for everything," said the *Oil and Gas Journal* in a November 1992 editorial. "An industry victory would mean real change in a nation that desperately needs to rediscover its ability to turn natural riches into human progress.…It would show appreciation for the benefits of domestically produced petroleum to economic growth, to the balance of trade, to employment, to security.… Whatever the odds, industry must fight this battle to the end."

Conservationists, as one of them put it in the late 1980s, have "drawn a line in the tundra" to keep North Slope oil development off the 1.5-million-acre coastal plain. With habitat supporting more than 200 species of animals, the coastal plain is considered the biological heartland of the refuge. It is considered critical habitat for the productivity of the Porcupine caribou herd; birds from six continents flock here to nest and raise their young. On a broader

FACING PAGE: A backpacker fords Marsh Fork of the Canning River in the Philip Smith Mountains of the western Arctic Refuge, part of he lands to the west and south added in 1980 when the original Arctic National Wildlife Range was doubled in size and made into the Arctic National Wildlife Refuge. (Dennis Miller)

Former President Jimmy Carter and his wife, Rosalynn, watch birds with Debbie S. Miller, at left, during the Carters' first visit to the Arctic National Wildlife Refuge in 1990. A decade earlier in one of his last official acts, President Carter signed the Alaska National Interest Lands Conservation Act that set aside more than 100 million acres in Alaska for national parks, preserves, wilderness areas and wildlife refuges, including the Arctic Refuge. Parts of the Carters' visit to the refuge were filmed for a television documentary about President Carter. (Dennis and Debbie Miller)

scale, the coastal plain symbolizes the fight to save for future generations what they see as the nation's last intact arctic ecosystem and one of America's greatest wildernesses.

"You don't take your wilderness areas…to the pawn shop for a quick shot of domestic oil," said Republican Sen. William Roth of Delaware in January 1993 as he introduced a wilderness bill to permanently protect the coastal plain from development. "Drilling for oil in the Arctic refuge is neither common sense nor environmentally sound." Added co-sponsor Sen. Claiborne Pell, a Democrat from Rhode Island, "Exploring for oil in this priceless wilderness is a sucker's bet."

It is not simply a battle of development versus conservation. Alaska Natives have lived in this corner of Alaska for centuries and continue to depend on it for food. The Natives have become players in the debate, with the Inupiat Eskimos of Kaktovik and the Gwich'in Athabaskan Indians of Arctic Village taking opposite sides of the issue.

Congress appeared ready to open the coastal plain to oil exploration several times in the late 1980s. Each side unleashed record levels of energy and spending to mobilize public support and take their case to lawmakers. But since November 1991, when senators opposed to drilling blocked an oil leasing bill from a vote on the floor, the fight has largely dropped from public view.

Now the question likely to emerge under Democratic President Bill Clinton, an opponent of oil leasing, is whether Congress will extend permanent wilderness protection to the coastal plain, a designation wanted by conservation groups.

▲ ▼ ▲

Americans have been arguing about this chunk of Alaska practically since the 1920s, when the federal government first set aside part of the North Slope for Navy oil and gas exploration. Almost from the start, conservationists began seeking wilderness protection for an expanse of the arctic slope and Brooks Range, a region containing the highest glaciated peaks in arctic North America, countless river valleys seen by few people, and a diversity of undisturbed habitats from boreal forests on the southern flank of the mountains to windswept marshes along the icy Beaufort Sea.

While the military wanted to tap the region's petroleum potential, others saw Alaska as the nation's last natural heritage, a place where indigenous people and animals lived much as they had for centuries.

"There is just one hope of repulsing the tyrannical ambition of civilization to conquer every niche on the whole earth. That hope is the organization of spirited people who will fight for the freedom of the wilderness," wrote Wilderness Society founder

Robert Marshall who made the first formal proposal for an Alaska arctic wilderness.

Among other things, the conservationists worried about military activity scarring the tundra. In 1943, the Department of Interior doubled the size of the Navy's petroleum reserve on Alaska's

BELOW LEFT: *An arctic fox, in its white color phase, stretches and yawns on the coastal plain. Its white winter camouflage will be replaced by brown fur during spring molt, and it will move to its summer breeding ground in the tundra. Arctic foxes spend their winters along the coast and on the sea ice where they may follow polar bears to scavenge remains of seal kills. These foxes are trapped for their fur in winter by Kaktovik residents. (Gary Schultz)*

RIGHT: *Polar bears in the Beaufort Sea region of Alaska give birth in dens on pack ice and land, with most of the land-based dens on the coastal plain of the Arctic National Wildlife Refuge. Between 1981 and 1992, U.S. Fish and Wildlife Service biologist Steven Amstrup found 44 polar bear maternity dens on the mainland coast of Alaska and Canada, with 20 of the dens within the refuge and 15 within the 1002 area of the coastal plain, an area of great interest to the oil industry because of its presumed petroleum potential. (Chlaus Lotscher)*

coastal plain to reach from Canada's coast west to Cape Lisburne. World War II spurred a decade-long petroleum exploration program conducted by the Navy and supported by U.S. Geological Survey mapping.

After the war but while the Navy was still searching for oil, the National Park Service began surveying Alaska's recreational resources. Senior park service planner George L. Collins, who headed the survey, sought advice from senior Geological Survey officials familiar with the Arctic. One of them, John C. Reed, told Collins to focus east of the Canning River, away from most of the oil explorations.

"The scenery was enthralling…simply stupendous, beyond description, absolutely magnificent," Collins recalls in John Kauffmann's *Alaska's Brooks Range* (1992). He and biologist colleague Lowell Sumner advanced a park proposal in 1954. They recommended leaving the area open to mineral activity, possibly to defray opposition.

Prominent conservationists, such as Olaus and Margaret Murie,

began building support for an even more restrictive wilderness designation.

None of this pleased politicians and business people in Alaska. They had already worked nearly a decade toward gaining self-governing powers through statehood, to escape federal oversight. Among other things, they wanted the Navy's petroleum reserve released for public leasing. They did not want more land tied up in a park or wilderness, particularly given that the conservationists wanting the arctic wildlife wilderness included those who opposed statehood. Acting manager Al Anderson of the Alaska Development Board joined territorial Gov. Frank Heintzleman in protests.

By 1959, when legislation reached Congress to create the Arctic

The annual migration of Porcupine caribou to the coast of the Arctic National Wildlife Refuge is one of the continent's great natural spectacles. The Porcupine caribou have figured prominently in the decades-long debate over oil development on the refuge's coastal plain, an area that includes the herd's primary calving grounds. (Gary Schultz)

National Wildlife Range, the Territorial Department of Mines charged that the proposed range represented "an effort to create a 9-million-acre playground at the expense of possible industrial development."

In congressional hearings held in seven Alaska cities, 73 residents testified in favor and 53 against the range. Alaska's senators successfully blocked Congressional authorization, yet the 8.9-million-acre Arctic Range was created by public land order by Interior Secretary Fred Seaton in 1960. The range would be open to mineral activity only with Congressional authorization. He then released about 20 million acres of the Navy's petroleum reserve to public mineral leasing.

The compromise did not satisfy Alaska's development proponents. Alaska's senators successfully blocked funding for the new range for the next nine years.

In the meantime, Alaska achieved statehood and as part of its land entitlement selected more than 1.8 million acres of the newly released coastal plain between the petroleum reserve and the Arctic Range. In 1968, four years after the first state oil lease sales, a major oil strike occurred at Prudhoe Bay, 65 miles west of the range.

Suddenly Congress found itself trying to settle pending Alaska Native land claims, so construction of an oil pipeline could proceed. The Alaska Native Claims Settlement Act (ANCSA) of 1971, which created regional and village Native corporations with endowments of federal land and money, contained provision Sec. 17 (d) (2), calling for 80 million acres of federal lands in Alaska to be made into parks and refuges.

The fight over the Arctic Range intensified. Conservationists wanted it enlarged under the "d-2" legislation. Alaska's senators pushed to open the range to oil development. Twice in the late 1970s, the House of Representatives voted to make the coastal plain of the refuge a wilderness. The emotional debate culminated in 1980 with the Alaska National Interest Lands Conservation Act (ANILCA), which created the Arctic National Wildlife Refuge and 15 other national wildlife refuges in the state.

The new Arctic Refuge included the original range plus 10 million acres to the south and west, although not as much as conservationists wanted. Congress extended wilderness protection to most of the original range, but bowed to development pressures and did not extend wilderness to the 100 miles of coastal plain between the Canning and Aichilik rivers.

Instead, it authorized a study of the coastal plain's oil and gas potential, as well as its wildlife resources under ANILCA Sec. 1002. From that point on, this 1.5-million-acre coastal region became known as the "ten-o-two" study area.

▲ ▼ ▲

In the years since, the 1002 area has become one of the nation's most intensely monitored wildlife habitats. Likewise, confrontations between development interests and preservationists have escalated.

Five years of extensive wildlife studies and several seasons of geological surface and seismic mapping on the 1002 area followed passage of ANILCA. The final 1002 Legislative Environmental Impact Statement issued in 1987 stands today as the most comprehensive overview of what could happen on the coastal plain.

The 1002 report found 26 major structural prospects, or geological formations capable of trapping oil and gas, and gave oil companies a 19 percent chance of finding petroleum in economically recoverable amounts. The odds were very promising by industry standards.

The assessment came from seismic and surface data. Only one well has been drilled within the refuge, 14 miles southeast of Kaktovik over what is thought to be the largest prospect. This well was drilled by the Arctic Slope Regional Corp., the ANCSA regional corporation, following a controversial land swap in 1983.

The regional corporation traded its land around Chandler Lake in Gates of the Arctic National Park for the coastal plain subsurface estate. The General Accounting Office criticized the Interior Department for allowing the swap and letting ASRC and oil company partners Chevron and BP Exploration drill and keep the findings secret. Congress later passed legislation prohibiting land exchanges in the Arctic Refuge without its approval. The state Supreme Court has since ruled that the state Dept. of Natural Resources oil and gas commission may

The only oil well inside the Arctic National Wildlife Refuge was drilled here, on Kaktovik Inupiat Corp. inholdings within the 1002 study area, by the Arctic Slope Regional Corp. and its partners in the venture, Chevron and BP Exploration. Results from the KIC well are confidential. This 1991 photo of the well site was taken five years after drilling was completed. No further drilling will be allowed, unless Congress opens the area to oil leasing. (Pamela A. Miller)

review the test well data but shall keep it confidential.

While the oil industry rallied behind the government's assessment of the coastal plain's petroleum potential, conservationists zeroed in on the report's findings that oil exploration and development would have adverse impacts.

In the case of exploration with no producing wells, the report said scars of seismic trails and well pads would remain for several years; an unknown number of small spills would cause ground and water pollution; wildlife would be temporarily displaced in some areas; and the Inupiat Eskimos would encounter short-term disruption in the subsistence use of the area.

Projected impacts from full oil development were more numerous. They included: direct loss of some 5,650 acres to road, drilling pad and gravel quarry sites, with another 7,000 acres affected by gravel spray, dust, altered snowmelt and erosion; numerous small oil spills; diversion of limited freshwater to industrial use; unquantifiable loss of wilderness values; possible reductions in musk ox, caribou, snow geese, wolves and polar bears from habitat losses; loss of up to 37 percent of the core caribou calving ground.

At the end of the exhaustive, 200-page report came Interior Secretary Donald Hodel's recommendation. In a two-paragraph conclusion, he determined "an orderly oil and gas leasing program for the entire 1002 area can be conducted in concert with America's environmental goals."

▲ ▼ ▲

Momentum built in Congress during the late 1980s for oil leasing. It fit the pro-development climate of the Bush administration. The oil industry, through the American Petroleum Institute and the Alaska Oil and Gas Association, intensified its efforts to sway public and political opinion. So did wilderness advocates, networking through The Wilderness Society, the Sierra Club and other conservation and environmental groups.

The rhetoric, spending, lawsuits and lobbying increased to previously unseen levels. The conservation coalition charged the oil industry with lax and environmentally damaging practices at Prudhoe Bay. The industry defended its practices, while expounding on new and superior technology, such as diagonal drilling, that it said would allow more compact and less intrusive development occupying less than 1 percent of the coastal plain. Alaskans were bombarded with oil company television commercials showing, among other things, caribou grazing in the shadow of oil rigs at Prudhoe Bay. The industry points to growth in the Central Arctic caribou herd, from 3,000 animals in 1975 to roughly 20,000 in 1990, as proof that oil and wildlife can coexist.

The Central Arctic herd ranges west to the Colville River, and east to the Tamayariak River, which lies inside the refuge. Its two main calving areas are along the Kuparuk River in the vicinity of the Kuparuk oil field developments and in the vicinity of Bullen Point, about 25 miles west of the Canning River.

Biologists with the U.S. Fish and Wildlife Service say efforts at Prudhoe Bay to mitigate the effects of development on the caribou may serve as a useful model if leasing is someday allowed on the coastal plain. But they caution against using the Central Arctic herd

Patches of aufeis mark channels of several rivers flowing north and south from the Brooks Range in the Arctic Refuge. (Chlaus Lotscher)

to make predictions about how development would impact the Porcupine herd, which is eight times larger with a more extensive migration pattern than the Central herd.

Each side also aligned themselves with the Alaska Natives. The Gwich'in Indians of Arctic Village depend almost entirely on the Porcupine caribou herd for food and culture and oppose any intrusion, such as oil drilling, that could adversely affect the herd.

The Inupiat Eskimos, who have shared in the wealth of North Slope oil, generally endorse opening the refuge to leasing. Inupiat subsistence depends much more on bowhead whales and other marine mammals than wildlife on land, although they take many caribou when available. They strongly oppose offshore oil activities because of possible disruptions to the whales, and would rather see the industry occupied on land.

The Eskimos of Kaktovik, the closest village to the refuge, own ground within the refuge and might benefit economically from oil activities. Individuals in Kaktovik vary in their opinions; some endorse exploration and development for its potential benefits. Others are outspoken against drilling because they hunt and fish

on the refuge and do not want their traditional use disrupted by access restrictions or possible industrial pollution. The village and regional government, for the record, support it.

In 1989, the Senate appeared poised to pass a bill to allow leasing. But the *Exxon Valdez* shipwreck, which spilled nearly 11 million gallons of North Slope crude oil into the Gulf of Alaska, killed further action on the bill.

The outbreak of war in the Persian Gulf in 1991 brought the matters of energy independence and national security to bear in a renewed oil leasing debate. Proponents pointed to declining production at Prudhoe Bay, the nation's most prolific field accounting for nearly 25 percent of domestic production, and emphasized the

The abandoned homestead of Ed Owens, a trapper and prospector who lived here with his family during the 1960s, sits in the timber country of the refuge on the south side of the Brooks Range. Privately owned parcels inside the refuge, known as inholdings, can be used, developed and sold similar to real estate elsewhere. Some people think that inholdings pose a threat to the refuge's wilderness values. (Gil Mull)

need to develop this promising new prospect to keep Alaska's pipeline humming. A drilling authorization was included in the Bush administration's comprehensive energy package. As in the earlier debates, Alaska officials supported leasing; North Slope oil production funds about 85 percent of the state's budget.

About the same time, the Interior Department upped the probability of finding recoverable oil on the coastal plain to 46 percent, based on new and reinterpreted geologic and geophysical data, changes in economics and engineering advances. The Wilderness Society challenged the revision in court, and the judge ruled against the Interior Department on several points.

As the bill neared floor action in the Senate, various interests once again kicked into high gear. On Nov. 1, 1991, senators opposing oil leasing mounted a filibuster and blocked a vote on the issue. Louisiana Sen. Bennett Johnston, who managed floor action on the bill, said, "The environmental groups…wrote the textbook on how to defeat a bill such as this, and my admiration is to them for the political skill which they exhibited."

▲ ▼ ▲

The future of the Arctic Refuge remains a question. The election of President Clinton brought for the first time in 12 years an administration opposed to leasing on the coastal plain.

Conservation-minded lawmakers introduced coastal plain wilderness bills in both houses of Congress almost as soon as Clinton took office. In the early months of his administration, observers cautiously predicted nothing would happen with coastal plain wilderness legislation, partly because there are more pressing conservation matters to address, such as reauthorization of the endangered species, marine mammals and clean water acts.

As long as Congress does not open the coastal plain to oil leasing, a seemingly unlikely scenario under Clinton, it is defacto wilderness.

In Alaska the newly formed pro-industry group Arctic Power quietly is organizing members for the next round. "If we sit around and do nothing, it is going to end up wilderness," says Debbie Reinwand, executive director. "But now is not the time to go full bore. We'll hold our fire until we have a target."

In the meantime, the U.S. Fish and Wildlife Service is completing additional studies of caribou, musk ox, polar bears, snow geese and other animals that use the coastal plain. They are trying to pinpoint the unique coastal plain features important to the animals. For instance, caribou feed on nutritious cottongrass, which blooms early and grows in abundance on the coastal plain. They also are trying to determine if there are other equally good but unused habitats outside the plain. Summaries of these studies are contained in a 400-page interim report with final reports expected by 1995.

Meanwhile oil industry, state and federal biologists are looking at Prudhoe Bay as a possible model for reducing impacts of oil activities should they ever be allowed on the coastal plain. Conflicting opinions among project members have delayed a final report.

▲ ▼ ▲

The attention of recent years has brought a dramatic increase in visitors to the refuge. This wildland now faces a new crisis, a threat of perhaps being ruined by its own popularity.

Refuge managers are developing a river management plan to deal with a dramatic increase in recreational users during the past decade. As Congress debated whether to allow oil leasing, people hurried to see firsthand what all the fuss was about.

In 1975, only one commercial outfitter had a permit to operate in the range, although several others without permits were bringing in groups. But by 1989, 21 outfitters offered backpacking and river trips. Rivers like the Hulahula and Kongakut have become increasingly congested during the short summer season. River usage increased from 702 visitor use days in 1984 to 5,063 visitor use days in 1991. A visitor use day is counted as one person using an area part or all of a day.

Likewise, air traffic into and out of the refuge has increased. Small bush planes buzz overhead, landing on gravel bars and lakes as they ferry backpackers and river rafters between the refuge and Arctic Village, Kaktovik or Fort Yukon, where most outfitters start and end their trips. Helicopters operating under special use permits

Steve Wakeland cooks a grayling on a stick during a backpacking outing in the Sheenjek Valley, among the most popular recreation areas within the refuge. (William Wakeland)

transported dozens of tour groups to the refuge during the oil leasing debates. These groups included members of Congress and their staff, national and international news crews, oil industry representatives and their allies including in some cases local politicians, and conservation group leaders and their allies.

While the tours have dwindled with no action pending in Congress, the refuge's popularity with wilderness adventurers continues. Suggestions by refuge users — hunters, backpackers, river rafters and Natives — range from doing nothing to limiting groups in size and access, from establishing subsistence-only corridors to no-fly zones.

Clearly, the oil leasing debate dominates the politics of the Arctic Refuge. But while it lies temporarily dormant, attention shifts to whether the wilderness values that have made the refuge so acclaimed can be maintained.

Bibliography

Alaska Geographic. *North Slope Now.* Anchorage: Alaska Geographic Society, 1989.

Bliss, Lawrence C. and Karen Gustafson. *Proposed Ecological Natural Landmarks in the Brooks Range, Alaska.* Seattle: Department of Botany, University of Washington, March 1981.

Collinson, Sir Richard. *Journal of the H.M.S. Enterprise.* New York: AMS Press, 1976.

Cook, John A. *Pursuing the Whale.* Boston: Houghton Mifflin & Co., 1926.

Franklin, Sir John. *Narrative of a Second Expedition to the Polar Sea.* New York: Greenwood Press, 1969.

Garner, Gerald W. and Patricia E. Reynolds, eds. *Arctic National Wildlife Refuge Coastal Plain Resource Assessment: Final Report Baseline Study of the Fish, Wildlife, and Their Habitats.* Volumes I and II. Anchorage: U.S. Department of Interior, U.S. Fish and Wildlife Service, Region 7, December 1986.

Isto, R.E. "Mount Michelson, Brooks Range," *American Alpine Journal.* New York: The American Alpine Club, 1958.

Jacobson, Michael J. and Cynthia Wentworth. *Kaktovik Subsistence, Land Use Values through Time in the Arctic National Wildlife Refuge Area.* Fairbanks: U.S. Fish and Wildlife Service, Northern Alaska Ecological Services, 1982.

Kauffmann, John M. *Alaska's Brooks Range, The Ultimate Mountains.* Seattle: The Mountaineers, 1992.

Kessel, Brina and George Schaller. *Birds of the Upper Sheenjek Valley, Northeastern Alaska.* Biological Papers of the University of Alaska, #4. Lancaster, Pennsylvania: The Intelligencer Printing Co., 1960.

Leffingwell, Ernest De K. *The Canning River Region, Northern Alaska.* United States Geological Survey, Professional Paper 109. Washington, D.C.: U.S. Government Printing Office, 1919.

Miller, Debbie S. *Midnight Wilderness: Journeys in Alaska's Arctic National Wildlife Refuge.* San Francisco: Sierra Club Books, 1990.

Milton, John P. *Nameless Valleys, Shining Mountains.* New York: Walker and Co., 1969.

Murie, Margaret E. *Two in the Far North.* Edmonds, Washington: Alaska Northwest Publishing Co., 1978.

Stefansson, Vilhjalmur. *My Life with the Eskimo.* New York: Macmillian, 1913.

Stuck, Hudson. *A Winter Circuit of our Arctic Coast.* New York: Charles Scribner's Sons, 1920.

U.S. Department of Interior. *Arctic National Wildlife Refuge, Alaska, Coastal Plain Resource Assessment: Report and Recommendation to the Congress of the United States and Final Legislative Impact Statement.* Prepared by the U.S. Fish and Wildlife Service in cooperation with U.S. Geological Survey and Bureau of Land Management, April 1987.

U.S. General Accounting Office. *Federal Land Management: Chandler Lake Land Exchange Not in the Government's Best Interest.* Report to the Chairman, Subcommittee on Water and Power Resources, Committee on Interior and Insular Affairs, House of Representatives, October 1989.

Photographers

DEATH OF A LANDMARK
(see page 90)

Wildlife and Alaska's Old-Growth Coastal Forest

BY BRUCE H. BAKER

EDITOR'S NOTE: *A forest resource consultant and freelance writer, Bruce recently completed 11 years as deputy director of the Alaska Department of Fish and Game's Habitat Division. He had previously spent 12 years with the U.S. Forest Service. For more information on the old-growth environment see* Timber Harvest and Water Quality in Alaska *(1991) by Alexander M. Milner, prepared for the U.S. Environmental Protection Agency by the University of Alaska, Arctic Environmental Information and Data Center; and "Wildlife and Old-Growth Forests in Southeastern Alaska," by John W. Schoen, Matthew D. Kirchhoff and Jeffrey H. Hughes in* Natural Areas Journal 8(3): 138-143.

These old-growth trees on Admiralty Island are large enough to intercept snow, allowing deer to move about and feed on the winter food plants present. Their roots also help stabilize the stream bank and may provide denning sites for furbearers. When the trees die and fall into the stream, they help create riffles and pools that are essential for survival of juvenile salmon. (John Schoen, courtesy of Bruce H. Baker)

During the 13,000 years or so since ice covered most of Alaska's moist Gulf Coast, a complex old-growth forest ecosystem has evolved to which myriad species of wildlife have adapted. What is this old-growth rain forest, and why is it so valuable for wildlife?

The coastal forests that extend from northern California to the southern Kenai Peninsula and the Afognak-Kodiak island group are variable in their tree species composition. They, nevertheless, share a damp, maritime climate in which fire is rare and is generally quite localized when it does occur. Western hemlock and Sitka spruce are common throughout most of this coastal forest system. Less abundant conifers in coastal Alaska include mountain hemlock, Alaska yellow cedar, western redcedar in the southern half of southeast Alaska, and the bonsai-like shore pine common to muskegs. Deciduous, broadleafed trees include black cottonwood that thrives in large river valleys and three species of alder that flourish in forest openings where the mineral soil has been exposed enough to the sun for seedlings to become established. Alder is one of the first trees to come in following glacial retreat and landslides, and its association with root-inhabiting mycorrhizal fungi allow it to fix atmospheric nitrogen, thus enriching otherwise nitrogen-impoverished soils.

Unlike Alaska's northern forests of white and black spruce, birch, and aspen, which owe much of their existence to recurring and extensive fires, the state's coastal forests are not generally subject to sudden and widespread tree mortality. As a result, they regenerate themselves through the replacement of individual trees or groups of trees that die or are blown down in heavy winds. The scattered openings in the dense forest canopy enable sunlight to reach the forest floor, promoting the establishment and growth of herbaceous ground plants such as bunchberry and fern-leaf goldthread, and shrubs such as blueberry — all of which happen to be important food plants for Sitka black-tailed deer. The result is a forest in a state of dynamic equilibrium in which a single acre can support ground plants, shrubs, and trees ranging in age from seedlings to those typically in excess of 300 years and sometimes more than 800 years. Large spruce can be 7 to 8 feet in diameter and 200 to 225 feet tall. It is this mosaic of forest vegetation on which coastal wildlife populations have come to depend.

THE SITKA BLACK-TAILED DEER

The habitat requirements of deer have been intensively researched along the northwest coast. In Washington and Oregon where most low-elevation, old-growth timber was harvested in the first half of this century and where snow rarely occurs in low-elevation winter habitat, deer have been able to find more forage in clear-cut areas than in the region's extensive second-growth forests. In coastal Alaska, however, Sitka black-tailed deer are at the northern limit of their range and deep snow at low elevations becomes

Of all of Alaska's wildlife species, perhaps the animal most closely associated with old-growth forest is the Sitka black-tailed deer. Many deer do not survive severe winters even with the best of habitat. This photo was taken at Hawk Inlet on Admiralty Island. In 1982, two-thirds of the deer collared by the Alaska Department of Fish and Game in this area did not survive the winter. (Mark Wayne)

a limiting factor in determining the size of deer populations. The combination of a partially sunlit forest floor where food plants can thrive, and the presence of large trees that can intercept enough snow to allow deer to move about with relative ease is essential for deer survival. Even under these most favorable conditions, deer mortality during severe winters can run high. According to Matt Kirchhoff, Alaska Department of Fish and Game biologist in Southeast, there are about 250,000 deer in the region with an estimated annual winter mortality of 10 percent to 75 percent. Wildlife biologists have

also found that important food plants growing among large trees have a higher nutritional content than do plants of the same species growing in large forest clearings created by humans.

OTHER MAMMALS AND BIRDS

Deer are not the only ungulates or hooved mammals that rely on old-growth in coastal Alaska. Although mountain goats are normally associated with habitats above timberline, they commonly seek out old-growth timber as refuge from severe winter storms that sweep nearby alpine ridges and summits. Even moose seek the

protection of old-growth during deep snow conditions.

Unique among the 50 states, Alaska's coastal old-growth forests still support in abundance the same complexes of prey and predator species that existed prior to Russian settlement. Predators such as the brown bear and the wolf have not fared well in the wake of extensive natural resource development elsewhere in the northern hemisphere. Many brown bears in coastal Alaska use the root cavities of large, high-elevation old-growth trees as winter den sites and depend for their survival on the abundant runs of salmon spawning in streams that wind through lower elevation timber. To the extent that their prey species depend on old-growth habitats, so too do bears and wolves.

Brown bear populations occupying old-growth timber are also less vulnerable to the depredation by humans that is usually associated with roads and forest clearings resulting from human activity. Although sport hunting pressure can be effectively regulated to compensate for improved physical access, an increase in the number of bears illegally killed or killed to protect life or property cannot be. To minimize the number of nuisance bears that are killed, it also becomes necessary to effectively dispose of garbage around centers of human activity. This is more easily achieved where human presence is limited and highly controlled, such as a mining operation, than it is in a larger and less disciplined community.

Furbearers depend on Alaska's coastal forests in a variety of ways. River otter and mink commonly den in stream banks that are stabilized by the roots of large trees, and marten feed on the red-backed voles and mice found in old-growth timber. The wolverine can be overexploited as areas are opened up by roads, and increased regulation of its harvest may be necessary to maintain populations in areas where human access is improved.

At least two dozen species of birds are associated with old-growth in Southeast, including breeding populations of hawks, owls and birds such as woodpeckers and chickadees that live in the cavities of dead trees. Even Vancouver Canada geese are known to occasionally nest in large spruce. Old-growth timber is also thought to provide important nesting habitat for marbled murrelets. Of the more than 7,000 bald eagles that inhabit Southeast, most construct nests near the shoreline in trees with an average age of more than 400 years.

Pink salmon return to spawn along Anan Creek on the Southeast mainland near Wrangell Island. Old-growth forests help stabilize salmon spawning streams, debris from the trees forms riffles and decaying debris helps replenish nutrients. (John Hyde)

FISH

All five species of commercially important salmon in Alaska — king, coho, sockeye, pink and chum — are produced in old-growth forest streams. Research in Southeast has shown that the presence of large, old trees growing within 100 feet of streams fulfills essential habitat functions. The roots of living trees provide bank and channel stability. Trees that die and eventually fall into the stream provide the large woody debris that is necessary to form pool and riffle habitat. The presence of living and dead wood in the stream bank and bed help prevent sedimentation and turbidity that would adversely affect fish. Insects, foliage and small branches that fall from overhanging trees are a source of nutrient replenishment for life in the stream. The forest canopy also has a modulating effect on extremely low winter temperatures and on the increased biological oxygen demand that can result from especially high summer temperatures. The forest canopy sends appreciable volumes of water vapor into the atmosphere through evaporation and transpiration from foliage, and this can help modulate extreme stream discharge peaks in the watershed, thus tempering the effects of flooding.

FOREST MANAGEMENT IMPLICATIONS

Fortunately, most of the benefits that riparian old-growth trees provide can be maintained by leaving timber along watercourses, and recent federal and state legislation provides a measure of protection. In 1990, Congress passed the Tongass Timber Reform Act requiring "a buffer zone of no less than one hundred feet in width on each side of all Class I streams in the Tongass National Forest, and on those Class II streams which flow directly into a Class I stream." Class I streams are those providing habitat to anadromous fish, those returning from the sea to their natal streams to spawn. Class II streams are generally steep and affect the quality of fish habitat in Class I streams.

State legislation, also passed in 1990, provides for the partial retention of timber within 66 feet of either stream bank on private forest lands. The state law also requires that on state-owned coastal forest land, "harvest of timber may not be undertaken within 100 feet immediately adjacent to an anadromous or high-value resident fish water body" and that "between 100 and 300 feet from the water body, timber harvest may occur but must be consistent with the maintenance of important fish habitat."

It is one thing to protect fish habitat by retaining old-growth timber along streams. It is more difficult to satisfy the old-growth requirements of other wildlife because they are not confined to such narrow corridors. Research in Southeast and elsewhere has

demonstrated the need to maintain a diversity of habitats for most wildlife populations to flourish. The variety of habitats required to provide such diversity varies among animal species. For example, the habitat requirements of mountain goats are clearly not the same as those for deer. Biological research has also indicated the need to avoid undue habitat fragmentation by ensuring that the different habitats required by an animal population are connected in a way that they can be effectively used and so that populations of the same species can intermingle over time, thereby maintaining a healthy gene pool. A challenge to land managers is to adopt an ecosystem

management strategy that prevents or minimizes undue habitat fragmentation as the land and timber base is allocated to a variety of human uses and land ownerships.

Another way to maintain wildlife populations is to ensure that habitats created through human activity serve the same functions as those that existed prior to human manipulation. In the case of Alaska's coastal old-growth forest, this would involve the creation of second-growth stands that emulate the characteristics of old-growth. Although biologists and land managers continue to investigate this as a potential partial solution, it has not been demonstrated to date that

old-growth habitat characteristics can be recreated in second-growth forests to a degree that historic populations of wildlife can be maintained.

The Tongass National Forest comprises more than 90 percent of the land base in Southeast, and one third of this forest is classified as commercial forest land. Of this, only 4 percent of the land base (672,000 acres) is classified as high-volume timber — supporting at least 30,000 board feet per acre. Less than 1 percent of the entire land base on the national forest (114,000 acres) occurs in the highest volume class, consisting of more than 50,000 board feet per acre.

For centuries, the harvest of trees by Alaska's Native people had a minor impact on this land. Trees could be used for long houses, canoes, totems and other local uses with no appreciable impact on wildlife habitats. In the years following Russian settlement, timber use increased, and by early this century so-called handlogging — the harvest of selected trees, usually close to the water — and other localized logging operations were taking place. It was not until the middle of this century, however, that widespread

Mountain goats rely on old-growth forest for shelter during severe storms. The state has 23,000 to 24,000 mountain goats, with the bulk of the population in Southeast, especially in Misty Fiords. (Pat Costello)

This 150-year-old second-growth stand lacks trees large enough to intercept the amount of snow necessary to let deer move about during severe winters. Also, there is not enough sunlight for important deer food plants to survive. (John Schoen, courtesy of Bruce H. Baker)

industrial-scale timber harvest became established in Southeast. Since 1950, more than 50 percent of the highest volume stands in Tongass National Forest, those exceeding 50,000 board feet per acre, have been logged. Of the remainder, 50 percent will be logged in the next 40 years under the current schedule. Ironically, the higher the timber volume per acre, the more valuable the forest is in providing winter deer habitat and the more attractive it generally is to the timber industry. During the period 1980 through 1986 alone, the average timber volume per acre that was harvested from the Tongass was more than

54,000 board feet. Federal and state biologists conclude that recent and anticipated levels of timber harvest on the Tongass forest will significantly reduce forest habitat diversity and populations of old-growth-dependent wildlife species, a point acknowledged in federal environmental impact analyses. Biologists have indicated that it takes most of 200 years for second-growth forests to begin to assume old-growth characteristics. They point out that as long as second-growth, replacement stands are themselves scheduled for harvest after approximately 100 years, the old-growth forest is a non-renewable natural resource.

Given the lack of legal protection on private forest lands for wildlife habitat other than anadromous fish, the amount of old-growth habitat that is reserved on state and national forest land will in large measure determine the future productivity of the region's wildlife populations throughout the next century and beyond.

A challenge to Alaskans is to understand the effects that timber harvest is likely to have on future wildlife populations and to make informed decisions as to what combinations of timber use and wildlife use can realistically be sustained indefinitely into the future. There are several federal laws that direct the protection of fish and other wildlife habitat on Alaska's two national forests. The implementation of these laws through a systematic land management planning process that involves an informed public is the key to protecting as much of coastal Alaska's old-growth forest habitat as possible. This will be a difficult challenge given the growing demand for competing natural resources that results from the world's ever-expanding human population.

The Arrow Points North

BY RICHARD P. EMANUEL

EDITOR'S NOTE:
A frequent contributor to ALASKA GEOGRAPHIC®, *Dick is a former hydrologist with the U.S. Geological Survey.*

When anthropologist Frederica de Laguna was about 13, she recalls, she wrote to arctic explorer Donald MacMillan, "begging to be allowed to go with him" on his next voyage to the frozen north.

Having read that Eskimo women chewed animal skins to soften them for use as clothing, she "offered to chew his boots if he would let me come. I remember crying bitterly when his polite refusal came."

More than 70 years after MacMillan declined the offer of his

The Anthropological Life of Frederica de Laguna

In 1932, Frederica de Laguna and her field crew explored Yukon Island off the south shore of Kachemak Bay. From left are students Bill Newman and Dana Street; Frederica de Laguna; her mother, Grace, with cat; and Jack Fields. Fields, from Seldovia, had shown de Laguna the Yukon Island and other important sites around Cook Inlet. According to historian and archaeologist Janet R. Klein, of Homer, Jack Fields and Harry Lewis owned the Dime, a 36-foot gas boat that de Laguna hired for archaeological site surveys. Fields is remembered as a friend to the Natives of Port Graham and English Bay, and was a licensed big game hunter who later turned away from hunting. Originally from Missouri, Fields left Seldovia about 1946 and returned to the Midwest. (Frederica de Laguna photo, from the collection of Janet R. Klein)

young admirer, the explorer is long dead. De Laguna's hair is gray and her step is careful, but her inner fire is undimmed and her love of the distant north is alive and well.

At 86, Frederica Annis de Leo de Laguna is among the most celebrated of living American anthropologists. She retired from Bryn Mawr College, in Pennsylvania, in 1975, after founding the school's anthropology department and teaching for 37 years. The same year, she and

Pilot Howard Reed, of Maritime Helicopters, flew anthropologist Frederica de Laguna around Kachemak Bay in April 1993 to revisit sites she had explored more than a half century earlier. (Janet R. Klein)

Margaret Mead became the first women anthropologists elected to the National Academy of Sciences.

De Laguna was in Anchorage in April 1993 to address an anthropological meeting and receive a lifetime achievement award. While in Alaska, she conferred with colleagues in Anchorage and Fairbanks and revisited the Kachemak Bay scene of her first Alaska triumph.

Born in Michigan in 1906, de Laguna moved as a baby to Bryn Mawr, outside Philadelphia, where her parents were philosophy professors. Her father was entranced by arctic lore and adventure and his copies of Elisha Kent Kane's 19th century *Arctic Explorations* (1856) and Vilhjalmur Stefansson's *The Friendly Arctic* (1915) fired

Frederica's mind, too. At her father's urging, after graduating from Bryn Mawr in 1927, she entered Columbia University, where Franz Boas and Ruth Benedict were inspiring a generation of anthropologists.

More than anything she encountered in book or classroom, arctic field work forever hooked de Laguna on anthropology. During a year abroad in 1929, she found herself in Copenhagen, examining Greenland Eskimo artifacts and conferring with Danish scientists. Among them was Therkel Mathiassen, a tall, fair Dane who fit the image of a Nordic explorer, according to de Laguna's memoir written in 1929 and published in 1975, *Voyage to Greenland: A Personal Initiation Into Anthropology*.

"I'd been in Denmark one week and Mathiassen was taking me through the museum," de Laguna recalls. Enthusiastically, he outlined plans for an archaeological survey of Greenland. "I said, 'Oh! I'd give anything to be able to go north on something like that.' And he said to me, 'Then come as my assistant.'"

For the next six months, de Laguna was "in seventh heaven." She excavated frozen burial sites and refuse heaps, observed Eskimo culture and sampled native foods. Her memoir, published 46 years later, abounds with accounts of boating through icy seas, climbing mountains and reveling in the long twilight glow of summer days in the Arctic. "I feel as if I could never be

content with ordinary living again," she later wrote to her parents, "unless it were to be broken by a return to the Arctic."

Her summer in Greenland shaped de Laguna's personal life as well as her career. En route to America, she visited her fiance, a mining engineer in a Welsh coal mine. She doubted, she wrote in *Voyage to Greenland*, that she could ever be the kind of wife that D__ expected, "So in the spring I sadly sent him back his ring." She remained unmarried.

De Laguna first traveled to Alaska the following year, in 1930. Still a graduate student, she scouted archaeological sites in Prince William Sound for a Danish anthropologist. Her younger brother accompanied her. With little to guide her, she booked passage to Cordova. "Perhaps the printing of the name Cordova was bigger than that of Latouche or Valdez," she says.

Upon arrival, she "toodled around to the office of the Regional Forester. Lee Pratt was his name, great big man, fine smile marred only by a couple of broken teeth, as I recall. I asked him for a permit to build a fire and he just about killed himself laughing. He was tipped back in his swivel chair and he nearly went over. He said, 'If you can get a fire to burn in this place, more power to you!'"

Having recovered his composure, Pratt turned out to be a helpful man. He suggested possible archaeological sites and took de Laguna and her brother in a boat to look several over.

Another useful tip came from the U.S. Marshal in Cordova, who directed her to a handful of Eyak Natives in the old village outside of town.

De Laguna visited the Eyak and gathered notes on their vocabulary, enough to confirm that they spoke a language distinct from their Chugach, Tlingit or Ahtna neighbors. Having run out of time on her first visit to Prince William Sound, de Laguna and her brother moved on to Cook Inlet. There, she hoped to track the culture that had produced a beautiful and mysterious lamp in the collection of the University of Pennsylvania Museum.

The lamp, for burning animal fat or oil, was an Eskimo design. It was about 16 inches long, carved of stone, a bowl with a seated human figure like an island within it. "When it was filled with oil," de Laguna says, the figure "would be submerged up to his waist with his big hands spread out in front of him."

The lamp had been found near Fish Creek in Knik Arm of Cook Inlet by a Finnish potato farmer. "This was outside the known Eskimo territory," de Laguna explains. The question arose whether Eskimos had once occupied Knik Arm.

De Laguna and her brother skiffed up the arm and dug fruitlessly near Fish Creek, Knik and Eklutna. Her brother then had to return to college but de Laguna chartered a gas boat from fisherman Jack Fields. He led her to a beach on Yukon

Island in Kachemak Bay, where he had found a skeleton wearing a bead necklace, and to a site on Cottonwood Creek on the northeast side of the bay.

Pay dirt! They dug up part of a lamp like the one that had started their quest. Subsequent excavation revealed that it came from a previously unknown Eskimo whaling culture in lower Cook Inlet. The Kachemak culture dates to before 1000 B.C. and predates prehistoric Athabaskan Indian sites around Kachemak Bay. Other lamps were later discovered. The one found near Knik may have been carried north as a prize of war.

The sheen of de Laguna's triumph was tarnished on her way home when she learned that her father had died in Vermont of a stroke on the very day she had found the Kachemak lamp. The following summer, her widowed mother joined in the renewed search for Cook Inlet's antiquities.

Early June 1935 found Frederica de Laguna, then 28, on the banks of the Tanana River, in Nenana. She planned to float down the Yukon River with an anthropological assistant and two geologists, scouting for archaeological sites left behind by late ice-age hunters.

The Yukon River valley was largely ice-free during the last ice age, between glaciers in the Brooks Range to the north and Alaska Range ice fields to the south. For people who had crossed the Bering land bridge,

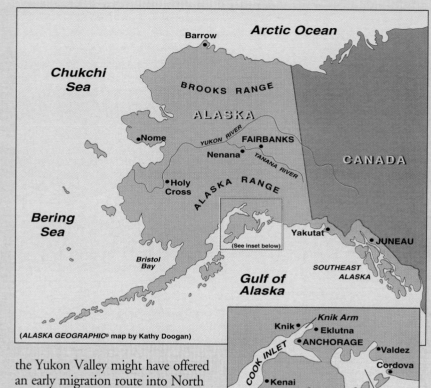

(ALASKA GEOGRAPHIC® map by Kathy Doogan)

the Yukon Valley might have offered an early migration route into North America. The scientists would seek signs of such a migration.

The first thing the party did in Nenana was to assemble a pair of skiffs. Late on the eighth day, the boats were ready and loaded, riding low in the water. The scientists gazed into the silvery sky of an Alaska Interior evening, then clambered aboard and shoved off into the river. Swiftly the current seized them, de Laguna recalls, "just like that and zip, around the corner and we were in a completely different world, civilization had really vanished. That was really thrilling!"

The thrill of that summer adventure has stayed with de Laguna for nearly 60 years. "One of the things that impressed me so much was the scent of the wild roses along the way and all the willow catkins floating down the river. It was just thick with them."

She long ago wrote an archaeological account of the trip,

In this 1949 photo taken at Angoon on Admiralty Island in Southeast, Frederica de Laguna wears the ceremonial regalia of the Raven Basket Bay Beaver clan. (Edward Malin; from the collection of Janet R. Klein, printed with permission of Frederica de Laguna)

which turned up disappointingly few signs of early man. Now she is writing a pair of popular books based on the journey. One will present myths and stories told to the anthropologists by Athabaskans in villages along the Yukon. A companion volume will relate the river trip: digging mammoth bone and ivory from a cliff face, the missionary who smashed the party's last bottle of wine, the flight from Holy Cross with bush pilot Noel Wien.

After 1935, events kept de Laguna from Alaska for 15 years. The Depression made jobs and funding scarce. Partly for money but more for amusement, she penned a pair of novels for the Doubleday Crime Club. *The Arrow Points to Murder*

appeared in 1937, followed by *Fog On the Mountain* (1938) set in a thinly veiled Seldovia. During the war, Lt. Cmdr. de Laguna served in Naval Intelligence, on the Alaska and German desks.

In 1949, de Laguna began a major study of the Tlingit of Southeastern Alaska, combining archaeology with ethnographic and historical studies of living Tlingit communities. Yakutat became the focus of her interest and she produced in 1964, with Francis A. Riddell and other members of the archaeological team, a report on the *Archaeology of the Yakutat Bay Area, Alaska*, followed in 1972 by her major work, *Under Mount Saint Elias: The History and Culture of the Yakutat Tlingit*, a three-volume model of multifaceted scholarship.

In 1955, the American Museum of Natural History asked de Laguna to edit a manuscript on the Tlingit by U.S. Navy Lt. George Thornton Emmons, who spent time among the Tlingit in the late 19th century. She agreed, "thinking it would be a very pleasant, not too difficult bookish task." After 36 years of intermittent wrestling with Emmons' notes and materials, the book emerged in

1991, to professional acclaim. In the interim, de Laguna collaborated with Dr. Catharine McClellan of the University of Wisconsin to study the Ahtna of the Copper River valley. A scholarly book on the Ahtna is now well along.

"I really do have a very ambitious program," de Laguna concedes. Then again, what seems optimistic in a woman of her age may be doable for de Laguna. Her philosopher mother lived to within a half-year of her hundredth birthday.

De Laguna recently moved her office from a basement on the Bryn Mawr campus to a room in her nearby apartment. To make space for her reference books and computer, she packed up her science fiction collection, and "most of my detective stories." You will still find a World War I-era entrenching tool in the trunk of her Plymouth car.

Perhaps in one respect only, de Laguna feels out of step with most anthropologists today. The trend in all science is to specialize, but de Laguna favors a broad approach. Archaeological artifacts, surveys of living cultures, language, myths, folk music, geography, food and art — all is grist for the open mind. De Laguna has always felt that the anthropologist should have no wastebasket, she says, just "a bigger and better filing system."

Ever the consummate anthropologist, in her long lifetime of living, nothing has ever been wasted by Frederica de Laguna.

Mardy Murie Film Project

A major television film project currently underway examines the life of Margaret E. "Mardy" Murie, matriarch of the conservation movement in the United States.

The biographical film focuses on her Alaska adventures, particularly those with Olaus Murie, her late husband and a founding director of The Wilderness Society. The Muries played a leading role in creation of the Arctic National Wildlife Range, and her continued efforts after his death helped bring about the larger Arctic National Wildlife Refuge.

The film will draw from historical footage made during the Muries' expeditions, still photos, and more than nine hours of "unique and often amazing footage of Mardy," says project and film director Bonnie Kreps. At 90, Mardy remains busy at her ranch in Moose, Wyo. This recent footage includes Mardy's reunion at the ranch last winter with Brina Kessel, Bob Krear and George Schaller, the scientists who accompanied the Muries to the Sheenjek Valley in 1956.

The Mardy Murie Film Project was publicly launched in February 1991 in Washington D.C. during Celebrate Wild Alaska! for the 10-year anniversary of the signing of the Alaska National Interest Lands Conservation Act. Kreps said her collaborator is Charlie Craighead, son of well-known bear biologist Frank Craighead.

For more information, please contact Bonnie at Mardy Murie Film Project, P.O. Box 153, Moose, Wyo. 83012.

EDITOR'S NOTE: Carla is a science writer for the Geophysical Institute at the University of Alaska Fairbanks.

Houseflies seem to mysteriously transcend Alaska's cold. Give them a little heat, and they'll behave in January as if it were August. Earlier this winter, an acquaintance heated up an outbuilding that had been chilled to minus 20, and found the place buzzing with dozens of thawed-out flies within just a few hours.

Many northern insects remain dormant through bitter cold, then come to life as soon as temperature permits. Arctic woolly bear caterpillars can stay frozen solid, at temperatures down to minus 58 degrees, for as long as 10 months without damage. Our multilegged denizens aren't the only ones to master the freeze-thaw life cycle. It's possible to find frozen frogs burrowed into the equally frozen mud in some Interior lakes.

Normally, freezing is deadly for living things. Ice crystals burst through cell and capillary walls, disrupting delicate structures at all levels from subcellular to whole organs. Even when freezing doesn't rip and break an organism, it provides other stresses. No fluid flow means no transfer of oxygen and no disposal of wastes, problems that usually mean no life.

Some animals get around these problems by operating internal furnaces — the technique mammals use — and growing furry or fatty protections against the cold. Cold-blooded animals, the exotherms, don't have that option. Many instead use variants on the antifreeze theme, producing chemical protectants that keep ice from forming in their body fluids just as antifreeze keeps water from freezing in a car's cooling system. Polar marine fishes are full of antifreeze, and so are many cold-adapted insects. This evolutionary adaptation means their life-sustaining fluids can be supercooled, staying liquid at temperatures below those at which they should freeze.

The antifreeze chemicals in the fishes and many northern spiders, mites and insects are proteins that block the effects of ice nucleators, particles that provide binding sites where water molecules begin the

How Alaska Insects Survive the COLD

BY CARLA HELFFERICH

Some caterpillars and other northern insects have surprising survival skills. Many have evolved an antifreeze system, which enables them to survive winter's cold. This moth caterpillar was photographed near Sadlerochit Spring in the Arctic National Wildlife Refuge in June, when snow still covered 30 percent to 40 percent of the ground. (David G. Roseneau)

process of setting up the orderly lattices of ice crystals. Nucleators turn out to be important also to the animals that get through the cold months by freezing solid. Their chances of surviving freezing are better if ice growth begins in the fluids not contained within cell membranes, such as urine or blood plasma. They are also better off if the freezing proceeds slowly and the crystals formed are small, as in good ice cream. To accomplish these ends, the animals synthesize nucleating agents when external cues trigger the process, such as declining temperatures and day length. The nucleators provide binding sites for the ice lattice formation to begin, and help set off the freezing process in the right

places and at the right speeds to produce the safer kinds of crystals.

Little ice crystals tend to agglomerate into bigger ones, as happens in ice cream stored too long. To prevent that, animals that freeze solid also produce enough antifreeze to block the refreezing of little crystals into bigger ones.

Many freeze-tolerant animals also produce other useful chemicals known as cryoprotectants, substances that protect cell structures and membranes against various effects of chilling. The cryoprotectants regulate cell volume during freezing and also seem to protect vital proteins and enzymes from the denaturing effects of very low temperatures.

Finally, the cells and organs of frozen animals are capable of surviving for a long time without oxygen. As their metabolic rates drop to 1 percent to 10 percent of their normal resting rates, their needs for energy and waste removal drop accordingly.

So, our winter-surviving creepers and buzzers are little less than chemical and physical marvels, capable of survival feats well beyond human capacities. 🐝

Pacific Storms Destroy Japanese Sailing Landmark

BY RICK MOSSMAN

EDITOR'S NOTE: *I first heard about the buried schooner on Manby side from Yakutat fisherman Rudy Pavlik while we boated among the islands of Yakutat Bay in 1977. When National Park Service ranger Rick Mossman mentioned in early 1993 that the sea had finally claimed the sailing ship, I asked if he wouldn't agree to tell readers the intriguing history of the trio of masts protruding from Schooner Beach.*

What is that, a ship? It's awful close to shore. That's how it appeared as

It took more than 80 years, but the sea finally destroyed the Japanese schooner Satsuma Maru, *shipwrecked on the Malaspina forelands in 1906. For decades the ship lay buried under varying amounts of coastal sand, but severe storms in 1990 and 1991 finally exposed the schooner to the constant pounding of waves that caused its final breakup. (Vincent Soboleff, Alaska State Library photo PCA 1-555)*

I hiked along the beach in Wrangell-St. Elias National Park, west of Yakutat, the first time in 1989. Before me I could see three straight poles sticking out of the sand, perhaps the masts of a buried ship. As it turned out, that is exactly what they were. For 82 years those masts had been sticking out of the sand. For more than four score years those masts were the only clue that a ship lay buried here. Locals from Yakutat remember as children swinging from the rigging, and that beach grass grew from the sand blanket covering the ship.

As the new Yakutat District Ranger for Wrangell-St. Elias National Park, I decided to investigate. After a check of office files and more research, I began to unravel the mystery.

The schooner was named the *Satsuma Maru* after its owner Tokujuo Satsuma of Osaka, Japan. The ship was built in 1906, and left Yokohama harbor on its maiden voyage in June of that year under the watch of Capt. Yasuzo Fujii. The ship was ordered to Alaska Territory to buy salmon. It arrived at Killisnoo, just south of Angoon on Admiralty Island's west coast, on Aug. 16, 1906. Because the *Satsuma Maru* had arrived too late for the salmon season, it took on a load of fertilizer (bird guano).

On October 16 the ship set sail for Japan, 12 days later she reached Yakutat Bay in a storm. On October 30 the captain decided to pull anchor and head for a sheltered bay near the town of Yakutat on the bay's southeastern shore. But the winds were against the ship, and the captain was forced to set anchor in 75 feet of water approximately five miles east of Point Manby in Yakutat Bay. The storm raged for several days, and on the

LEFT: *Capt. Robert McGillivray, of the steamer* Jeanie, *received a scarlet ribbon and silver medal from the Japanese government for his and his crew's efforts to rescue members of a Japanese crew shipwrecked on the Malaspina coast. Here the* Jeanie *is shown offloading cargo at Nome in 1901. (San Francisco Maritime National Historical Park, R.E. MacKay Collection, G2.2703n)*

ABOVE: *A chain and timbers from the stern are exposed by waves. (Rick Mossman)*

night of November 5 the stern and bow anchor chains broke, freeing the ship to float helplessly. The *Satsuma Maru* went ashore approximately three miles east of Point Manby.

Capt. Fujii frantically tried to get his 18-man crew and the ship's provisions ashore, losing in the effort one crewman who was washed into the sea. For the next three months, the sailors endured rain, snow and winter dark on the beach, surviving on the ship's provisions and what they could find along the shore. Another crewman perished during this time, and the captain could only contemplate his future because losing a ship mandated hanging under Japanese maritime law.

On Feb. 3, 1907, the captain and five of his strongest crew boarded one of the small rowboats from the *Satsuma Maru* and attempted to row approximately 20 miles to the settlement of Yakutat. After a "many days journey under arduous circumstances," they reached town and sought help. Five days later the steamer *Jeanie* called at Yakutat and agreed to attempt rescue. During the attempt, two more men were lost at sea. The rescue was aborted and the *Jeanie* returned to Yakutat.

Capt. Fujii sailed with the *Jeanie* to Seattle to obtain help from the Japanese Consul. U.S. authorities agreed to dispatch the Revenue Cutter *Thetis*, and Capt. Fujii returned with the *Thetis* to Yakutat. On March 3 the surviving crew members were rescued after spending four winter months on the isolated shore that is today known as Schooner Beach.

Capt. Fujii and his 10 remaining crew returned to Japan. At his trial in

January 1908, the captain was pardoned for his crime because the court ruled that "both anchor chains breaking at once was an act of God."

In March 1990, my interest in the *Satsuma Maru* peaked when, in a once-a-century phenomena, winter high tides eroded away approximately 5 to 6 vertical feet of sand along Schooner Beach and exposed for the first time in more than 80 years the deck of the *Satsuma Maru*. My duty was to document and record this new historic resource.

That same month, volunteers Bob Johnson, Julie Jackson Mossman and I flew to the site. As we investigated the ship, we were amazed at the remarkable preservation of the blocks and pulleys exposed with each new tide. They glistened in the sun and swung freely as if waiting for the captain once again to run up the rigging.

For three days we measured, photographed and videotaped the uncovering of the Japanese schooner. With each new tide, the beach gave way, subjecting the ship to the pounding of the surf. In April the bowsprit was torn lose, crushing many of the smaller pieces and breaking off the side rails and much of the exposed side ribbing. But by summer 1990, the ocean had redeposited sand along the beach and partially reburied the *Satsuma Maru*, postponing its final days a bit longer.

In April 1991, strong tides eroded away the beach again. The ship was now awash at high and low tides and constantly battered by the surf. By the end of April the waves had snapped the forward mast and part of the main mast.

By June nothing was left of the ship. The ocean had finally after nearly 85 years captured the *Satsuma Maru*.

BELOW: Timbers and gear for the rigging of the Japanese schooner survived for decades under the sands. (Rick Mossman)

RIGHT: National Park Service staff and volunteers document the remains of the Satsuma Maru. (Rick Mossman)

NATIONAL ARCHIVES-ALASKA REGION COLLECT THE PAPER OF ALASKA'S PAST

BY L.J. CAMPBELL

A cavernous room in downtown Anchorage contains the paper trail of Alaska's past, neatly filed in rows of gray boxes on tall metal shelves. Welcome to the inner sanctum of the National Archives-Alaska Region, the 12th and newest branch of the federal government's depository of official life.

The Alaska Region, at Third and G streets behind the historic Federal Building, opened September 1991. In the 18 months since, it has surpassed planners' most optimistic use projections. Its collections have grown faster than expected; already the records storage room is nearly half full. But more significantly, within a year of opening the region ranked second behind the New England Region in Boston in the number of people using the archives' collection of original papers, or textual materials.

"It's a satisfying benchmark," says Alaska Region Director Tom Wiltsey.

The Alaska Region archives hold the raw bones of Alaska's history — records, maps, letters, facts and figures, and obscure curiosities generated by federal agencies from as far back, in some cases, as 1867 when the United States bought Alaska from Russia. Most of the holdings date from the 1920s and '30s. The collections include 9,400 cubic feet of papers and 65,000 rolls of microfilm, many of which contain copies of records similar to those held in textual form. Almost half of

the rolls of microfilm are devoted to federal population censuses starting in 1790.

Located in the archives are court transcripts, agency reports, hand-written personal letters, blueprints and maps. There are records generated by agencies such as the Bureau of Indian Affairs, Bureau of Land Management, Fish and Wildlife Service, National Park Service and Forest Service. Material from Alaska's territorial days includes records from the Alaska Road Commission, the territorial and district courts, correspondence of territorial governors and legislatures, records from Alaska customhouses and annual reports of the Alaska Railroad. Alaska's maritime and military history appears in records from the U.S. Customs Service, the U.S. Coast Guard, the 17th Naval District and the Alaska Communications System.

Some materials are exceedingly dry in content. Others provide

intriguing word snapshots, like the 1949 letter from a German, Frederick Schuller, asking territorial Gov. Ernest Gruening for permission to settle in the Matanuska Valley. Or petitions from immigrants detailing their skin and hair color, distinguishing marks like scars and tattoos, and accounts of how they got here. Tucked away in the files from the Agricultural Experiment Stations in Alaska, 1891 to 1932, are tidbits about plant hybridization trials and pioneering efforts to grow tulips and gladiolus.

Some records lie in obscurity for years, tapped occasionally by the odd scholar trying to track some particular historical lead, says Wiltsey. Then suddenly, the same records are discovered to have real practical value. For instance, old Navy records now are getting frequent use by the Army Corps of Engineers and environmental groups trying to locate old ammunition dumps and fuel farms.

The Alaska Region's initial acquisition came with the transfer of Alaska-specific records from the National Archives-Pacific Northwest Region in Seattle. The bulk of the records — more than 20,000 boxes of them — arrived during summer 1991. Every week a barge from Seattle brought another 40-foot trailer-load of boxes that the staff unloaded onto a conveyor belt into the storage area.

It is a dizzying array, and it continues to grow. The land deed issued today, the annual report compiled this year, are tomorrow's archives. As records created by various federal agencies are no longer needed for daily business, they are moved into temporary storage at the Alaska Region. At some point, those records with historical value are given to the archives, moved across an aisle into permanent storage, and made available to the public. It is an ongoing cycle.

The Alaska Region's staff of four stay busy, tending to public research requests and preserving and cataloguing the endless paper flow. All the textual material goes into the heart of the archives, a large red-floored storage area called the stacks. The southeast corner of the stacks serves as the archivists' main work station, where they survey incoming material. They review each item and place it inside archival containers, typically acid-free folders inside acid-free boxes, to prevent further deterioration. A hydration chamber, looking like a set of shelves covered with an opaque plastic bag, sits nearby. Old maps and other rolled papers go into the chamber where moisture penetrates the fibers, allowing them to relax and unfurl. The items are then placed between blotters, weighted by acrylic panes to dry flat. Then they go into archival folders and map drawers.

The archivists' occasional conversations, in low tones befitting a library atmosphere, are muffled by the whirr of the ventilation system and swallowed by the stacks' vastness. The climate of the storage area is controlled. Air temperatures hover around 70 degrees, with about 50 percent humidity. The air moves through a charcoal filter and the

lighting is shielded with ultraviolet filters.

Each box is coded for a specific place on one of the numerous floor-to-ceiling shelves, or a particular cabinet. This way, the staff can more easily find items requested by people doing research. The stacks are off-limits to the public, separated from the outer public areas by double sets of locked doors.

The public areas include a small work room with tables for researchers, a microfilm room, a lobby with exhibits and a lecture-conference room.

With thousands of available records, zoning in on the right ones is a daunting challenge. "This is the raw stuff of history," says Wiltsey. "From this you can form your own opinions, your own interpretations... if you've got the time." The Alaska Branch provides a 22-page summary of its textual holdings and a lengthy cabinet-by-cabinet description of microfilms. Supplements are provided as needed to describe recent accessions. The federal census is indexed in 400 volumes, arranged by state with surnames listed alphabetically. Numerous guides covering various aspects of the entire National Archives system are also available. While most of the Alaska records from the Seattle region are now in Anchorage, other Alaska records remain at a few western regional branches and at the National Archives' main depository in Washington D.C.

Published by

**THE ALASKA
GEOGRAPHIC
SOCIETY**

Penny Rennick,
EDITOR

Kathy Doogan,
PRODUCTION DIRECTOR

L.J. Campbell,
STAFF WRITER

Kevin Kerns,
BUSINESS & CIRCULATION MANAGER

Patty Bliss,
CUSTOMER SERVICE REPRESENTATIVE

SPECTACLED EIDER JOINS LIST OF THREATENED SPECIES IN ALASKA

In spring 1993 the U.S. Fish and Wildlife Service (USFWS) officially listed the spectacled eider as threatened under the Endangered Species Act. Populations of this sea duck, known for its distinctive eye patch that resembles spectacles, are declining rapidly on the bird's primary breeding grounds on Alaska's west coast. Scientists have also noted a decline of spectacled eiders on other known breeding grounds such as along Alaska's arctic coast and in Russia.

The spectacled eider population has not been counted worldwide, and estimates of the population decline are based on studies within Alaska. USFWS biologists estimate the breeding population has declined from 50,000 or more pairs in the early 1970s to a few thousand pairs in the early 1990s.

Causes of the decline have not yet been identified, partly because much is still to be learned about this species, such as where the eiders spend most of their lives. After their short summer breeding season on the tundra of coastal Alaska and Russia, the birds leave for unknown wintering grounds. USFWS scientists plan to use satellite telemetry to learn if the winter feeding grounds for this duck are near the pack ice in the western Bering Sea, as suspected.

Additional studies will focus on surveys of breeding birds, and sources of mortality. Another project on Russia's Indigirka delta will provide a rangewide comparison for these Alaska studies. Biologists have not counted spectacled eider populations in Russia, although they estimate that perhaps 30,000 to 40,000 pairs nested along the Russian coast 20 years ago.

Alaska and Russia Natives have traditionally harvested spectacled eiders for food and clothing with no apparent effect on historic populations. The current estimated subsistence harvest in Alaska, based on voluntary reports, is at least 500 spectacled eiders per year. In 1992, the USFWS began a program to inform Alaskans living in the state's western and northern coastal areas about the plight of the spectacled eider and to encourage their cooperation with the no-hunting policy until the population recovers. As of summer 1993, USFWS policy called for no harvesting of spectacled eiders. (Photo by John Warden)

MAGNETIC NORTH, A TREK ACROSS CANADA FROM THE PACIFIC TO THE ATLANTIC BY FOOT, DOGSLED AND CANOE, by David Halsey with Diana Landau, Sierra Club Books, San Francisco, 252 pages, 13 color photos, 8 maps, bibliography, index of place names, hardcover, $19.95.

This book describes David Halsey's 4,700-mile journey across Canada, from Vancouver on the Pacific Ocean to Tadoussac, a town on the St. Lawrence River in Quebec. It chronicles two years of often-harrowing adventures.

Halsey envisioned his expedition as a wilderness crossing accomplished by primitive means in the fashion of the early explorers whom he admired. And so he did. He backpacked, snowshoed, dogsledded and canoed across high deserts, mountain forests, frozen tundra, churning rivers and stormy lakes. Some of the trip was solo; most included Chicago photographer Peter Souchuk and a stray coyote-dog named Ki.

Before the 1977 trip, Halsey amassed maps and accounts of historic explorations, tirelessly promoted his idea and finally dropped out of college as a sophomore to pursue his dream. He convinced the National Geographic Society to provide money, photographic equipment and consider the story for publication. He recruited team members through newspaper advertisements, meeting them for the first time in person a few days before the expedition started.

Four days into the trip, his companions angrily quit. They apparently were put-off by Halsey's attitude, and felt the expedition was poorly equipped and planned. They left Halsey alone on a river bank, taking most of the expedition equipment and supplies.

After quaffing a few beers in a Fort Langley pub and being assured over the telephone of his parents' moral and financial support, Halsey continued on. Having once bemoaned that previous outdoor experiences had never been strenuous enough for him to discover his "panic threshold," he embarked on a journey in which he would find his limit many times over.

His story, though lively and well-written, borders on being yet another tale of an inexperienced, ill-equipped adventurer taking foolish risks for no clear reason. For instance, he continues after his teammates' mutiny with no tent, no rope and little food. He disdained using a compass, perferring to rely on his sense of direction. In some ways, Halsey's experience is akin to bungee jumping, where people fling themselves from high bridges and are jerked to safety at the last minute by a tenuous rubber tether. Time and time, Halsey launches himself into the abyss, narrowly averting death by quick reflexes and luck.

Yet his honesty, in admitting shortcomings and mistakes, and his enthusiasm, for what he sees and learns, make him a sympathetic character. Plus, he is a quick learner. By the time Halsey meets up with Souchuk, the story is too compelling to quit. They survive frostbite, exposure, near-drownings and a few other assorted disasters and acquire many bush skills, often aided at crucial moments by the kindness of strangers.

Two sections are particularly interesting. One offers an insight into the current debate over minimal-impact camping. Halsey and Souchuk are resting after a brutal series of rapids on the Albany River. Along the way, they had marked portages with orange surveyor's tape, left caches of cigarette butts and used teabags, and in one place left a pair of torn pants. A group of American canoeists joins their camp downstream. The leader complains about the "crap in the wilderness" that they had had to clean up.

The encounter was typical of the contrast in attitudes and behavior between those who visited the northern bush for a few weeks and those who lived there...we tended to identify with the latter and adopt their methods.... This group of canoeists was seeking unspoiled wilderness, and the sight of our orange tape marking campsites was enough to spoil it for them. Maybe the next group would have felt likewise. Or maybe they missed a portage and had to cut their own trail...hack out a miserable campsite in the rain. Had they found one of our old camps, they could have calmed their panic with a coffee can full of hot tea and a relaxing smoke. I've done the same myself at old Indian camps...an Ojibway family...would have been delighted to find (the denim pants), and a patient seamstress could have extended their usefulness many months.

In national parks and wilderness areas stateside, I'm all in favor of picking up litter and leaving the place as you found it.... But it's not necessarily appropriate in a working environment like the northern bush, where you may travel for a month without meeting another soul....

Among the best told chapters are those detailing Halsey's winter with Cree Indian trappers at Lake River, an isolated camp about 300 miles north of the James Bay town of Moosonee. Halsey develops more self-sufficiency working a trap line alone while learning the traditional ways of his adopted Cree family.

While the expedition ended in success and Halsey triumphed over numerous setbacks in accomplishing his dream, his story has a sad ending. A few years after the trip and before he finished the book, Halsey died of a probable suicide. He was 26, and had been diagnosed as manic-depressive about six months earlier, and had started treatment, according to editor Diana Landau who completed the manuscript from his notes, drafts and letters.

— *L. J. Campbell*

ALASKA GEOGRAPHIC. *back issues*

The North Slope, Vol. 1, No. 1. Charter issue. Out of print.

One Man's Wilderness, Vol. 1, No. 2. Out of print.

Admiralty...Island in Contention, Vol. 1, No. 3. $7.50.

Fisheries of the North Pacific, Vol. 1, No. 4. Out of print.

Alaska-Yukon Wild Flowers Guide, Vol. 2, No. 1. Out of print.

Richard Harrington's Yukon, Vol. 2, No. 2. Out of print.

Prince William Sound, Vol. 2, No. 3. Out of print.

Yakutat: The Turbulent Crescent, Vol. 2, No. 4. Out of print.

Glacier Bay: Old Ice, New Land, Vol. 3, No. 1. Out of print.

The Land: Eye of the Storm, Vol. 3, No. 2. Out of print.

Richard Harrington's Antarctic, Vol. 3, No. 3. $12.95.

The Silver Years, Vol. 3, No. 4. $17.95.

Alaska's Volcanoes: Northern Link In the Ring of Fire, Vol. 4, No. 1. Out of print.

The Brooks Range, Vol. 4, No. 2. Out of print.

Kodiak: Island of Change, Vol. 4, No. 3. Out of print.

Wilderness Proposals, Vol. 4, No. 4. Out of print.

Cook Inlet Country, Vol. 5, No. 1. Out of print.

Southeast: Alaska's Panhandle, Vol. 5, No. 2. Out of print.

Bristol Bay Basin, Vol. 5, No. 3. Out of print.

Alaska Whales and Whaling, Vol. 5, No. 4. $19.95.

Yukon-Kuskokwim Delta, Vol. 6, No. 1. Out of print.

Aurora Borealis, Vol. 6, No. 2. Out of print.

Alaska's Native People, Vol. 6, No. 3. $24.95.

The Stikine River, Vol. 6, No. 4. $12.95.

Alaska's Great Interior, Vol. 7, No. 1. $17.95.

Photographic Geography of Alaska, Vol. 7, No. 2. Out of print.

The Aleutians, Vol. 7, No. 3. Out of print.

Klondike Lost, Vol. 7, No. 4. Out of print.

Wrangell-Saint Elias, Vol. 8, No. 1. $19.95.

Alaska Mammals, Vol. 8, No. 2. $15.95.

The Kotzebue Basin, Vol. 8, No. 3. $15.95.

Alaska National Interest Lands, Vol. 8, No. 4. $17.95.

Alaska's Glaciers, Vol. 9, No. 1. Revised 1993. $19.95.

Sitka and Its Ocean/Island World, Vol. 9, No. 2. $19.95.

Islands of the Seals: The Pribilofs, Vol. 9, No. 3. $12.95.

Alaska's Oil/Gas & Minerals Industry, Vol. 9, No. 4. $15.95.

Adventure Roads North, Vol. 10, No. 1. $17.95.

Anchorage and the Cook Inlet Basin, Vol. 10, No. 2. $17.95.

Alaska's Salmon Fisheries, Vol. 10, No. 3. $15.95.

Up the Koyukuk, Vol. 10, No. 4. $17.95.

Nome: City of the Golden Beaches, Vol. 11, No. 1. $14.95.

Alaska's Farms and Gardens, Vol. 11, No. 2. $15.95.

Chilkat River Valley, Vol. 11, No. 3. $15.95.

Alaska Steam, Vol. 11, No. 4. $14.95.

Northwest Territories, Vol. 12, No. 1. $17.95.

Alaska's Forest Resources, Vol. 12, No. 2. $16.95.

Alaska Native Arts and Crafts, Vol. 12, No. 3. $17.95.

Our Arctic Year, Vol. 12, No. 4. $15.95.

Where Mountains Meet the Sea: Alaska's Gulf Coast, Vol. 13, No. 1. $17.95.

Backcountry Alaska, Vol. 13, No. 2. $17.95.

British Columbia's Coast, Vol. 13, No. 3. $17.95.

Lake Clark/Lake Iliamna Country, Vol. 13, No. 4. Out of print.

Dogs of the North, Vol. 14, No. 1. $17.95.

South/Southeast Alaska, Vol. 14, No. 2. Out of print.

Alaska's Seward Peninsula, Vol. 14, No. 3. $15.95.

The Upper Yukon Basin, Vol. 14, No. 4. $17.95.

Glacier Bay: Icy Wilderness, Vol. 15, No. 1. Out of print.

Dawson City, Vol. 15, No. 2. $15.95.

Denali, Vol. 15, No. 3. $16.95.

The Kuskokwim River, Vol. 15, No. 4. $17.95.

Katmai Country, Vol. 16, No. 1. $17.95.

North Slope Now, Vol. 16, No. 2. $14.95.

The Tanana Basin, Vol. 16, No. 3. $17.95.

The Copper Trail, Vol. 16, No. 4. $17.95.

The Nushagak Basin, Vol. 17, No. 1. $17.95.

Juneau, Vol. 17, No. 2. $17.95.

The Middle Yukon River, Vol. 17, No. 3. $17.95.

The Lower Yukon River, Vol. 17, No. 4. $17.95.

Alaska's Weather, Vol. 18, No. 1. $17.95.

Alaska's Volcanoes, Vol. 18, No. 2. $17.95.

Admiralty Island: Fortress of the Bears, Vol. 18, No. 3. $17.95.

Unalaska/Dutch Harbor, Vol. 18, No. 4. $17.95.

Skagway: A Legacy of Gold, Vol. 19, No. 1. $18.95.

ALASKA: The Great Land, Vol. 19, No. 2. $18.95.

Kodiak, Vol. 19, No.˙3. $18.95.

Alaska's Railroads, Vol. 19, No. 4. $18.95.

Prince William Sound, Vol. 20, No. 1. $18.95.

Southeast Alaska, Vol. 20, No. 2. $19.95.

ALL PRICES SUBJECT TO CHANGE

Your $39 membership in The Alaska Geographic Society includes four subsequent issues of *ALASKA GEOGRAPHIC*, the Society's official quarterly. Please add $10 for non-U.S. memberships.

Additional membership information is available on request. Single copies of the *ALASKA GEOGRAPHIC* back issues are also available. When ordering, please make payments in U.S. funds and add $2.00 postage/handling per copy book rate; $4.00 per copy for Priority Mail. Non-U.S. postage extra. Free catalog available. To order back issues send your check or money order and volumes desired to:

The Alaska Geographic Society

P.O. Box 93370
Anchorage, AK 99509

NEXT ISSUE: *Alaska's Bears*, Vol. 20, No. 4. Three species of bears inhabit Alaska's wilderness areas. This issue details the natural history of brown/grizzly, black and polar bears, describes bear-viewing areas and records the adventures of some of the scientists who know these monarchs firsthand. To members 1993, with index. $18.95.